cooking for the week

cooking

LEISURELY WEEKEND COOKING FOR EASY WEEKDAY MEALS

for the week

by Diane Morgan, Dan Taggart, and Kathleen Taggart Photographs by Leigh Beisch

CHRONICLE BOOKS

SAN FRANCISCO

Library of Congress Cataloging-in-Publication Data:

Morgan, Diane, 1955–

Cooking for the week: leisurely weekend cooking for easy weekday meals/

by Diane Morgan, Dan Taggart, and Kathleen Taggart; photographs by Leigh Beisch.

p. cm.

Includes index.

ISBN 0-8118-2128-5

1. Cookery.   2. Cookery (Leftovers).   I. Taggart, Dan.

II. Taggart, Kathleen, 1951–.   III. Title.

TX715.M8435 1999

641.5—dc21

98–31674

CIP

Printed in Hong Kong.

Food Styling by Dan Becker

Prop Styling by Carol Hacker

For Dana for his unyielding support and for Dad for showing me how to see.—Leigh Beisch

For my mom for teaching me to eat.—Dan Becker

Designed by Level

Distributed in Canada by Raincoast Books

8680 Cambie Street

Vancouver, British Columbia V6P 6M9

10 9 8 7 6 5 4 3 2

Chronicle Books

85 Second Street

San Francisco, California 94105

www.chroniclebooks.com

To our respective mothers and grandmothers, who taught us the virtue of leftovers.

contents

WEEKEND MENU Broiled Flank Steak with Soy-Honey Marinade; Curried Roasted Potatoes; Oven-Baked Tomatoes; Mixed Fruit Compote

WEEKDAY MEALS Flank Steak, Potato, and Roasted Red Pepper Salad; Tomato-Bread Soup with Parmesan; Buckwheat Soba with Slivered Flank Steak, Green Onions, and Orange Zest

WEEKEND MENU Whole Roast Salmon; Lemon-Garlic Couscous; Crunchy Snow Peas; Chocolate–Chocolate Chip Biscotti

WEEKDAY MEALS Salmon Hash; Couscous Salad with Cashews, Currants, and Snow Peas; Risotto with Salmon, Parsley, and Green Onions

WEEKEND MENU Standing Rib Roast (Prime Rib); Classic Mashed Potatoes; Caramelized Onions and Carrots; Coffee Granita with Chocolate Sauce

WEEKDAY MEALS Potato Pancakes; Apple and Blue Cheese Salad with Pecans; Pasta with Porcini Mushrooms, Caramelized Onions, and Carrots; Paprika Beef with Mushrooms; Prime Rib Sandwiches

WEEKEND MENU Bourbon-Glazed Ham; Sweet Potato Sauté; Sautéed Swiss Chard; Cherry Pie

WEEKDAY MEALS Cheddar Macaroni with Ham; Ham, Shrimp, and Sweet Potato Jambalaya; Asian Noodle Bowl with Ham; Ham, Sweet Potato, and Swiss Chard Frittata

WEEKEND MENU Grilled Chicken with Herbed Mustard; Grilled Corn on the Cob; Grilled Zucchini and Summer Squash; Focaccia; Ice Cream with Raspberry Sauce and Sliced Peaches

WEEKDAY MEALS Spicy Corn Chowder; Chicken Quesadillas with Tomatillo Salsa; Focaccia Sandwich with Grilled Squash, Goat Cheese, and Basil

WEEKEND MENU Grilled Butterflied Leg of Lamb; Yogurt, Goat Cheese, and Sun-Dried Tomato Spread; Grilled Eggplant and Onion Slices; Pita Breads; Nectarine and Blueberry Crisp

WEEKDAY MEALS Lamb Curry; Lamb and Pita Sandwiches with Yogurt-Mint Sauce; Penne with Grilled Vegetables and Sun-Dried Tomato Sauce; Lamb and Roma Tomato Double-Crust Pizza

WEEKEND MENU Poached Halibut with Chipotle Sauce; Steamed New Potatoes; Stir-Fried Baby Bok Choy; Lemon–Poppy Seed Cake

WEEKDAY MEALS Halibut Tacos; Curried Fish Soup with Potatoes, Jalapeños, and Tomatoes

WEEKEND MENU Roast Breast of Turkey; Spicy White Bean Stew with Roasted Red Peppers; Walnut Bread; Pears Baked in Red Wine

WEEKDAY MEALS Bean Soup with Bacon and Oregano; Turkey Caesar Salad with Walnut Bread Croutons; Turkey Tetrazzini

acknowledgments

In essence, this book truly reflects our everyday cooking. For us, it is a joy to cook on a weekend when time permits. But it is an even greater joy to come home on a weeknight, from work or from chauffeuring the kids, knowing that dinner is at hand. To be able to write on this subject was all pleasure, and we are grateful for the support and encouragement we received. Elise and Arnold Goodman believed in this project from the start. Bill LeBlond offered sound advice, caring counsel, and thoughtful commentary—a writer couldn't ask for more. Sarah Putman kept us on track and we are grateful for her insights and guidance. Caroline Miller edited our work with sensitivity and thoughtfulness. It is always a thrill to receive the galleys and see what a terrific job the Chronicle Books design team has done.

Close to home we have always had recipe testers. They kept us on our toes with their frank comments and thoughtful questions. We are so grateful to David Berger and Bonnie Culberhouse for their continuous support and eagerness to test recipes. Others that were ready with knives and chopping boards were Margie and Ken Sanders, Kathleen Dintruff, Gary Nedelisky, and Faye and Scott Holman along with their daughters, Dominique and Samantha. Lloyd Irwin, Jim and Judy Rankin, Trisha Knepper, Jeff Swafford, David Taggart, Terry Burko, and Marianne Barber put on their aprons and tested away. Many thanks.

Greg Morgan has been a part of more cookbook meetings than he can count, yet his well-tuned palate and keen observations remain invaluable. Eric and Molly Morgan, their mom's harshest critics, never even knew they were eating leftovers.

Cooking for the Week is a book in praise of *intentionally* cooking more than you need for a single meal.

Good cooks know that extra cooked (and properly stored) food is not only inevitable; it is desirable. An empty refrigerator dooms the household chef to starting from scratch every time dinner (or lunch, or breakfast) is on the horizon. No one finds moldy mystery leftovers appealing, but the lack of any usable cold edibles simply means more work in the kitchen and duller, more repetitive meals.

Consider: A small leg of lamb might feed four persons adequately. A larger roast will too, and will also provide enough tender cold lamb to slice and stuff into pita breads with sliced tomatoes, shredded lettuce, and yogurt-mint sauce: a sandwich that will produce smiles all around the table. Consider, too: A grilled or pan-seared fresh tuna steak with, say, new potatoes and asparagus is a noble meal. So is, a couple of days later, a niçoise salad with olives and potatoes—especially if you don't have to cook tuna or potatoes a second time. Consider, also: A simple roast duck is a princely entrée of two or perhaps three portions. Two ducks provide the same original meal *and* enough succulent shredded duck to enrobe in warm soft corn tortillas along with a quick homemade tomato salsa: soft tacos so flavorful they nourish the mind as well as the body.

Our mission in this book is to encourage you to think more creatively in the kitchen. Food doesn't have to be served the same way twice in a row, and is usually more appealing if it is not. Meat, fish, and fowl—when served as a rehash of a former meal—nearly always arrive at the table drier than when they were served originally. A few minutes spent with a knife, cutting board, and a little imagination can result in a moist, tender chicken salad rather than over-dry reheated roast chicken, or deliver soba noodles with tender slivered flank steak instead of rewarmed flank steak as tough as shoe leather. A pork and Cheddar sub sandwich eclipses plain reheated pork; a creamy salmon risotto triumphs over desiccated coho. All the recipes in this book, whether weekend or weekday, are geared for four persons, and the weekend desserts will often do another round of duty later in the week.

Cooking creatively with cold cooked food requires mild skill with a kitchen knife or two, and a bit of imagination. We believe that a real cook can open the refrigerator, inventory its perishable contents, and come up with a plan for using them in an appealing way. A *smart* cook plans the whole thing in advance.

the pantry

A cook's best friend is the pantry, a term we use to include the cupboard, the refrigerator, and the freezer. Basic foodstuffs kept on hand are a boon to any cook. We can't imagine a cupboard without some cans of tomatoes, chicken broth, and tuna. Nor is it conceivable to find our pantry without fruity olive oil, rice, balsamic vinegar, and a bottle of soy sauce. A spare pound of butter in the freezer is always a help, as is a container of pesto. The narrow shelves of any refrigerator door happily will hold a couple of jars of mustard, some pickles and capers, and mayonnaise. But to help you think about building a pantry in a systematic way, we have devised some lists for you to follow. Know yourself as a cook and what you like to make; if baking is not your style then don't bother to have baking staples on hand. However, if you are wild about all things Italian, then by all means keep those shelves well stocked with pasta, Arborio rice, and polenta.

ON THE SHELF

Several cans low-salt chicken broth
Several cans whole Italian (plum) tomatoes
Tomato paste
Tuna
Canned black beans and small white beans
Canned tomatillos
Canned chipotle chilies
Unsweetened coconut milk
Oil-packed sun-dried tomatoes
Cured black olives
Capers
Anchovy paste
Bottled red pepper sauce (store in the refrigerator once opened)
Fruity olive oil
Vegetable oil
Vegetable-oil cooking spray
Balsamic vinegar
Unseasoned rice vinegar

Asian sesame oil (store in the refrigerator once opened)
Soy sauce
Dry sherry
Bottled clam juice
Dried porcini mushrooms
Dried black (shiitake) mushrooms
Short-grain rice
Long-grain rice
Arborio rice
Quick-cooking couscous
Polenta
Dried pasta such as spaghetti, linguine, penne, farfalle
All-purpose flour
Garlic
Yellow onions

Herbs, Spices, and Condiments
Salt
Black peppercorns
Bay leaves
Cayenne pepper (store in the refrigerator once opened)

Ground cinnamon
Cinnamon sticks
Ground coriander
Coriander seeds
Red pepper flakes (store in the refrigerator once opened)
Ground cumin
Cumin seeds
Curry powder
Dried dill weed
Dry mustard
Nutmeg
Dried oregano
Paprika (store in the refrigerator once opened)
Dried thyme

10

FOR THE BAKER	IN THE REFRIGERATOR
Granulated sugar	Milk
Powdered sugar	Large eggs
Light brown sugar	Parmesan cheese
Dark brown sugar	Cheddar cheese
Honey	Unsalted butter
Maple syrup	(keep an extra pound
Pure vanilla extract	in the freezer)
Vanilla beans	Solid vegetable
Baking powder	shortening
Baking soda	Dijon-style mustard
Cornstarch	Mayonnaise
Cornmeal	Carrots
Old-fashioned oatmeal	Celery
Unsweetened chocolate	Parsley
Semisweet chocolate	Lemons
Unsweetened cocoa	
powder	IN THE FREEZER
Semisweet chocolate	Active dry yeast
chips	Shelled walnuts
Raisins	Shelled pecans
Dried currants	Pine nuts
	Pesto
	Ice cream (!)

THOROUGHLY WASH YOUR HANDS, using hot water and hand soap, before touching food or utensils. Your own two hands are your best kitchen tool, and they pick up bacteria from everything you touch, so wash them often.

CUT RAW MEAT, poultry, or fish on a separate board using a separate knife. Or, if using one board and knife, prepare foods that are not to be cooked (such as salad ingredients) first and set them aside; then use the board and knife to cut raw meats, poultry, or fish.

SANITIZE WOOD CUTTING BOARDS after cutting raw meat, poultry, or fish by wiping with a solution of one teaspoon chlorine bleach mixed with one and a half cups water. Allow to air-dry. The chlorine kills most of the bacteria.

COOK POULTRY AND GROUND MEATS, such as hamburger, to 160°F.

COVER AND REFRIGERATE cooked foods within two hours of removing from heat. Cooked foods at room temperature offer a perfect breeding medium for bacteria to grow in. Place raw meats, poultry, and fish on lower shelves so they cannot drip onto other foods.

DON'T dry dishes with the same towel that you dry your hands with. Air-dry your dishes if possible. Kitchen sponges are notorious for bacterial content, so change them regularly. Anti-bacterial sponges are now in supermarkets.

READ THE RECIPE ALL THE WAY THROUGH a first time, which will help you discover whether something needs to be prepared in advance or you need equipment you don't have.

MEASUREMENT IS LISTED FIRST, THEN PREPARATION. For example, "½ cup lightly packed parsley leaves, chopped" means you first measure out the parsley leaves by lightly packing them into a measure, then chop them. It does not mean you will wind up with ½ cup of chopped parsley.

INGREDIENTS ARE LISTED in the order in which they are required once you start cooking.

CHICKEN STOCK is called for in many recipes, and you will find a recipe on page 23. We have listed canned low-salt chicken broth as an alternative.

COOKWARE SIZE AND SHAPE is specified. It is usually better to use a size larger rather than a size smaller if you need to make an adjustment.

HEAT LEVELS VARY widely between types of stovetops. If you feel that what you are doing requires higher heat on your stovetop, make the change.

SALT: This book assumes you are using granulated table salt unless otherwise noted. Don't add salt to a recipe that includes canned broth before you taste it, or you may create a disaster. If the liquid has been reduced at all, the broth's salt will have been concentrated.

MEASURING FLOUR: Stir, scoop, and sweep. Because flour settles and compacts, it should be spooned out of the bag into a measure and leveled off with a knife. If the flour is in a storage container, just use a whisk or fork to stir the flour to lighten it—you'll feel the difference—and then scoop flour using a dry-measure cup with a handle. Level the top with anything flat.

BUTTER: We use unsalted butter in all cases, because we can more precisely control the amount of salt in a recipe that way.

MEASURING INTERNAL TEMPERATURES OF FOODS: There is no substitute for an instant-read thermometer when you want to quickly know the temperature of a food or liquid. Insert the tip into the center of whatever you are measuring for an accurate reading. Don't leave one in the oven—most of them have a plastic dial that will melt.

MEASURING OVEN TEMPERATURES: Ovens vary significantly in their accuracy. Invest in a good oven thermometer, one with a spirit stem rather than springs, so that you will know how hot the oven really is.

HERBS: If you must substitute for fresh herbs, use one third as much dried herb.

"HOT PEPPER SAUCE" refers to bottled cayenne-and-vinegar-style sauces such as Frank's and Tabasco.

SEEDED means the seeds have been removed from peppers, chilies, or tomatoes.

There are literally dozens of brands and styles of outdoor grills on the market. Our recipes assume that you have either a kettle-style charcoal grill or gas or electric grill. Kettle grill cooking racks are usually not adjustable for height, so the heat level is determined by how much charcoal is being used and how long it has burned, and by controlling the position of lid vents. Charcoal can be added through the openings provided next to the rack handles on some grills; on others, you may need to lift the rack slightly to add fuel. Various grill-top accessories are available, one of the most useful being a rib rack, which holds several racks of ribs vertically. This allows the cooking of twice as many racks of ribs at one time.

We suggest using regular hardwood charcoal briquettes, not the presoaked kind. Chunk wood charcoal (rather than briquette style) is available in many locations. Our experience is that it burns hotter and longer. We prefer charcoal chimneys, which need only a page or two of newspaper to ignite charcoal quickly, or electric starters. If you use starter fluid, be certain the fire is uniformly hot before cooking, which will ensure that the lighter fluid has burned away. Never add fluid to burning coals!

To start a charcoal fire, open the vents on the bottom of the grill and mound about three pounds of charcoal in the center of the charcoal grate. Squirt starter fluid over the charcoal, and let soak for a minute. Light the charcoal. Or, use a charcoal chimney or an electric starter according to the manufacturer's directions. When the coals are covered with gray ash, spread them evenly over the charcoal grate, if using the direct-cooking method, or mound them to one or both sides of the charcoal grate, if using the indirect-cooking method.

A direct fire uses coals positioned directly below the cooking rack. It is employed to quickly grill foods that do not need long, slow cooking, such as hamburgers or fish steaks or fillets. An indirect fire uses coals mounded against one or both sides of the grill, with food positioned on the opposite side from the coals or between the mounds of coals. Some grills have special metal baskets positioned inside to hold charcoal in the correct position for indirect cooking. A drip pan is often positioned below food to prevent grease flare-ups. Indirect cooking is used particularly for long, slow cooking, as for barbecued ribs.

Judging how hot a fire is takes practice, but a time-honored method is to hold your hand five or six inches above the cooking grate and count off seconds—"one thousand one, one thousand two, one thousand three," and so on. If your hand is uncomfortable after one or two seconds, the fire is hot. If you can count three or four seconds, the fire is medium. If you can count five or six seconds, you have a low fire.

Most flavor in grilling comes when food juices drip onto the coals, producing smoke. An extra degree of smokiness can be produced by adding hardwood chips to a fire. An aluminum foil pouch folded around the chips, with a few holes poked in it, is a handy package to lay directly on coals. Or, use a small disposable aluminum pan. A couple of handfuls of chips are usually enough to get the job done.

A long-handled spatula and long-handled spring tongs are valuable grilling tools. The spatula helps prevent burns; the spring tongs make it easier to turn food on the grill. Use a heavy-duty natural bristle (not nylon) brush to oil the cooking rack before grilling.

weekend

ROAST CHICKEN WITH LEMON, GARLIC, AND FRESH ROSEMARY
HERBED DROP BISCUITS
STEAMED BROCCOLI
CHOCOLATE CHEESECAKE

monday

BISCUIT-TOPPED CHICKEN PIE
This takeoff on the old favorite, potpie, uses leftover chicken in a quick, creamy sauce with mushrooms. Popped into ramekins and topped with leftover biscuits, only a quick bake is needed.

wednesday

LINGUINE WITH BROCCOLI AND BLUE CHEESE
Pasta always makes a quick supper, and this one uses already-cooked broccoli.

thursday

ASIAN CHICKEN SALAD WITH GREEN ONION–SESAME DRESSING
This light and healthy salad uses the rest of the roast chicken along with sautéed cabbage, cellophane noodles, carrot, cucumber, and toasted sesame seeds.

We have a recipe for roast chicken in almost every cookbook we've written. And why not? It has to be one of the world's most satisfying dishes. In this case, we happily roast two chickens on the weekend so that great things can happen later in the week. The weekend meal is classic American fare: roast chicken flavored with lemon, garlic, and fresh rosemary. It is accompanied with some homemade biscuits filled with savory herbs and bright green steamed broccoli. A luscious chocolate cheesecake finishes the meal.

The meal itself is a snap to do. The only advance preparation is to make the cheesecake a day in advance, or very early the day of serving. The chickens roast for about an hour. Fifteen minutes or so before they are done, prepare the biscuits. Pop them in the oven to bake, and steam the broccoli while the chicken is resting.

Roasting an extra chicken provides two great weekday meals: a chicken pie and an Asian-style chicken salad. The extra broccoli becomes part of a yummy pasta dish.

Roast Chicken with Lemon, Garlic, and Fresh Rosemary

Makes 2 roast chickens, 1 to serve (for 4 people) and 1 reserved for Biscuit-Topped Chicken Pie (page 22) and Asian Chicken Salad with Green Onion–Sesame Dressing (page 25)

Roast chicken—a perfect Sunday night supper. Cook 2 birds for guaranteed leftovers. Butter, lemon, garlic, and rosemary flavor the birds, but the possibilities are endless. When blood oranges are in season, try substituting them for the lemons, leaving out the garlic and using fresh mint instead of rosemary.

2 whole fresh chickens ($4\frac{1}{2}$ to $4\frac{3}{4}$
   pounds each)
$\frac{1}{2}$ cup (1 stick) unsalted butter
   Juice of 2 lemons (quarter and reserve
   squeezed lemons)
4 garlic cloves, halved lengthwise
   Salt and freshly ground pepper to taste
6 sprigs fresh rosemary, each about
   3 inches long

Preheat the oven to 375°F. Remove the sacks of giblets from the chickens. Freeze the neck, heart, and gizzards for stock; fry the liver for a four-legged friend. Pull out and discard any large fat deposits from the cavities of the chicken. Trim any loose skin and trim off the tails. Pat dry with paper towels.

Line a large roasting pan with aluminum foil for easy cleanup, unless the pan is nonstick. Place a roasting rack or large wire cake rack in the pan. In a small saucepan, melt the butter. Add the lemon juice, garlic, salt, and pepper. Heat through.

Set the chickens on the roasting rack, breast-side up. Place 3 rosemary sprigs and 4 lemon quarters in each cavity. Brush the seasoned butter on the birds, coating them well. Place the roasting pan in the lower half of the oven and roast, basting every 20 minutes, until the juices run clear when a sharp knife is inserted into the joint between the body and thigh, or when an instant-read thermometer registers 170°F inserted at the same point, about 1 hour.

Remove the chickens from the oven, baste again, and cover loosely with aluminum foil. Leave 1 chicken to cool completely. Let the other chicken rest for 10 minutes, then carve and serve. Cut the other chicken in half, wrap each half well, and store in the refrigerator for up to 4 days.

Herbed Drop Biscuits

Makes 24 small biscuits, with 8 reserved for Biscuit-Topped Chicken Pie (page 22)

A staple in the American South for several hundred years, biscuits deserve to be made more often. They are delectable when served hot out of the oven, and are not difficult to make. This version includes fresh oregano, parsley, and sage, and goes very nicely with the roast chicken.

3 cups all-purpose flour

2 teaspoons baking soda

2 teaspoons baking powder

¾ teaspoon salt

7 tablespoons unsalted butter

¼ cup minced fresh oregano

¼ cup minced fresh parsley

¼ cup minced fresh sage

½ teaspoon freshly ground pepper

1¼ cups buttermilk

2 tablespoons olive oil for brushing

Preheat the oven to 425°F. In a large bowl, combine the flour, baking soda, baking powder, salt, and butter. Use a pastry cutter or your fingertips to work the butter into the flour until butter pieces are no larger than a pea. Add the herbs, pepper, and buttermilk, stirring just to blend well. Drop heaping tablespoonfuls of dough about 1 inch apart on an ungreased baking sheet. Brush the biscuits with the olive oil. Bake until lightly browned, 12 to 14 minutes. Set aside 8 biscuits to cool and serve the rest. Place the reserved biscuits in a lock-top freezer bag and freeze until needed for the potpie.

Steamed Broccoli

Serves 4, with half reserved for Linguine with Broccoli and Blue Cheese (page 24)

Former President Bush may have contributed more to America's nutrition than he knew by making a joke of his dislike for the vegetable. The truth is, broccoli is more popular than ever, is very good for you, and if you don't overcook it, has wonderful flavor and color. The key is watching the timing during cooking. Like other green vegetables, cooking it much more than seven minutes will result in color loss.

2 large bunches broccoli, about 4 pounds
2 tablespoons unsalted butter, melted

Trim the broccoli by cutting off the stalks about 2 inches below the florets and peeling away any tough skin. Cut into serving portions. Cook the broccoli in 2 batches, creating your leftovers first. Put half the broccoli in a steamer basket or a folding steamer and steam, covered, over boiling water until crisp-tender, 5 to 7 minutes. The broccoli may also be cooked in an uncovered big pot of salted boiling water. Transfer the broccoli to a big bowl of ice water for 5 minutes, then drain well. Cover and store in the refrigerator for up to 5 days.

About 7 minutes before you want to serve, cook the remaining broccoli. Drain the hot broccoli, put it in a serving bowl, and drizzle with the melted butter. Serve.

Chocolate Cheesecake

Makes 12 servings

Cheesecakes are not difficult to make and are uniformly popular. The simpler the meal, the better a cheesecake fits into the menu, we think. This one has a chocolate shortbread crust and is topped with sweetened sour cream and pecan halves for a handsome presentation. Plan to make it a day before serving, so that it is thoroughly cooled and set when you serve it.

Preheat the oven to 375°F. Spray a 9-inch springform pan (see Cook's Note) with vegetable-oil cooking spray.

CRUST:

½ cup (1 stick) unsalted butter at room
   temperature
½ cup granulated sugar
½ cup all-purpose flour
¼ cup unsweetened cocoa powder,
   preferably Dutch process
¼ cup cornmeal
⅛ teaspoon salt
¼ teaspoon ground nutmeg

TO MAKE THE CRUST: In a large bowl, cream the butter and sugar together with a wooden spoon or an electric mixer until light and fluffy. In a small bowl, whisk the flour, cocoa, cornmeal, salt, and nutmeg together. Mix into the butter mixture until blended. Using your fingers, press the mixture evenly into the bottom of the springform pan. Set the pan on a square of aluminum foil and pull it up snugly around the pan's sides to prevent butter from leaking out of the pan. Set in a baking pan and bake for 25 minutes. Remove from the oven, leave the foil-wrapped pan in the baking pan, and reduce oven temperature to 350°F.

FILLING:

1½ pounds cream cheese at room
   temperature
1 cup granulated sugar
4 large eggs
1 cup (½ pint) heavy (whipping) cream
8 ounces semisweet chocolate, chopped
¼ cup bourbon whiskey
1 tablespoon pure vanilla extract

TO MAKE THE FILLING: While the crust is baking, combine the cream cheese and sugar in a large bowl and beat until the mixture is light and thoroughly blended. Beat in the eggs, one at a time, just until incorporated. In a 1-quart saucepan, combine the cream and chocolate and cook over medium-low heat, stirring with a heatproof spatula, until the chocolate is completely melted. Add the bourbon, vanilla, nutmeg, and salt to the chocolate mixture. Pour into the cream cheese mixture, add the cornstarch, and beat until the batter is completely smooth. Pour into the pre-baked crust.

1 teaspoon ground nutmeg
¼ teaspoon salt
⅓ cup cornstarch

Bake at 350°F until the top center of the cheesecake just barely appears liquid when the pan is gently jiggled, 50 to 60 minutes. Remove from the oven and let cool for 20 minutes; leave the oven on.

TOPPING:

12 perfect pecan halves
2 cups (1 pint) sour cream
1 tablespoon granulated sugar
1 teaspoon pure vanilla extract

1 tablespoon unsweetened cocoa powder
  for dusting

TO MAKE THE TOPPING: Spread the pecans on a baking sheet and toast for 5 minutes; remove from the oven. In a medium bowl, whisk the sour cream, sugar, and vanilla together. When the cheesecake has cooled for 20 minutes, gently spread the sour cream mixture over the top, smoothing with a spatula. Return the pan to the oven for 5 minutes, then remove. Gently press the pecans around the top of cake about 1 inch inside the edge, positioned like numbers on a clock to mark the 12 slices. Let cool for 2 hours. Insert a toothpick in the center of the cheesecake and gently cover it with plastic wrap—the toothpick will hold the plastic wrap off the top of the cheesecake to preserve its beauty. Refrigerate for at least 6 hours, or preferably overnight.

Before serving, put the cocoa in a small fine-meshed sieve and gently tap it while holding it over the cheesecake to dust the top attractively. To serve, run a knife around the inside of the rim to loosen the cheesecake, then unlatch the rim and carefully remove. Cut slices with a warm, wet cake or carving knife, wiping the knife clean between slices.

COOK'S NOTE   *A springform pan has an expandable latched rim that can be easily removed. Look for one at a kitchenware shop.*

Biscuit-Topped Chicken Pie

Serves 4

We hope your memories from childhood include some homemade chicken potpie, not just frozen ones. Here is the perfect opportunity to use half a leftover chicken and some of the biscuits reserved from Sunday night's dinner.

1½ cups Chicken Stock (recipe follows) or canned low-salt chicken broth

1 medium carrot (4 ounces), peeled, cut in half lengthwise, then cut into ⅛-inch-thick slices

3 tablespoons unsalted butter

2 tablespoons vegetable oil

1 small yellow onion (about 4 ounces), peeled and diced

8 ounces white mushrooms, quartered

2 tablespoons all-purpose flour

½ cup heavy (whipping) cream

½ Roast Chicken with Lemon, Garlic, and Fresh Rosemary (page 17) skinned, meat cut from bones and cut into ½-inch cubes

½ cup minced fresh parsley

Salt and freshly ground pepper to taste

8 frozen Herbed Drop Biscuits (page 18)

Preheat the oven to 400°F. Set four 12-ounce ramekins on a baking sheet, or use an 8-cup baking dish about 2 inches deep.

In a 1-quart saucepan, bring the stock or broth to a simmer. Add the carrots and cook until crisp-tender, about 10 minutes. Using a slotted spoon transfer the carrots to a plate and turn off heat under the stock or broth.

Meanwhile, in a 10-inch sauté pan or skillet, melt the butter with the oil over medium heat until the butter foams. Add the onion and sauté until it begins to soften, about 2 minutes. Add the mushrooms and sauté until they just begin to brown, about 3 minutes more. Sprinkle the flour over the onion-mushroom mixture and stir to dissolve. Immediately add the stock or broth, bring to a simmer, and stir until smooth and thickened, about 2 minutes. Add the cream, stir to blend, and bring to a simmer. Add the chicken, carrots, and parsley, bring to a simmer, then add salt and pepper. Remove from heat.

Divide the chicken mixture among the ramekins or spoon it into the baking dish. Place 2 frozen biscuits on top of the chicken mixture in each ramekin, or evenly space them on top of the chicken mixture in the baking dish. Bake for 12 minutes, or until heated through. Serve immediately.

COOK'S NOTES *If you prefer potatoes in your potpie, skip the mushrooms and add a cubed peeled 8-ounce boiling potato to the stock or broth along with the carrots. Simmer for 10 minutes. Set aside and add to the pan along with the carrots. Parsnip would also be good. Follow the same procedure as for a potato. If you like peas, add ½ cup frozen peas when you add the chicken and parsley.*

Put the chicken carcass in a lock-top plastic bag, label it, and freeze it to save for making stock.

Chicken Stock

4 quarts (about 4 pounds) chicken parts
   (see Cook's Note)
1 medium unpeeled carrot
1 medium unpeeled yellow onion
½ rib celery, with leaves
½ teaspoon peppercorns
1 bay leaf
1 cup loosely packed fresh parsley leaves
   and stems

Select a heavy 4-quart saucepan or a 6- to 8-quart stockpot. Fill it with the chicken parts and add cold water to cover, leaving 2 inches of space at the top of the pan. Bring to a boil over medium-high heat, then reduce heat so that the liquid simmers steadily. Skim off the brown foam that rises to the top, using a soup skimmer, a small tea strainer, or a serving spoon. After 5 minutes or so the foam will become white; no more skimming is necessary.

Add all the remaining ingredients. Cover the pot loosely and adjust heat so that the liquid just barely simmers. Simmer the stock for 4 to 8 hours, adding water if necessary to keep the bones covered.

Using a slotted spoon, transfer the bones and meat to a colander or strainer set over a large bowl to catch all the juices. Discard the bones and meat and pour the drippings back into the saucepan or stockpot. Pour the stock through a fine-mesh strainer back into the large bowl, then back into the pan or pot. Set the pan or pot in a sink filled with cold water, changing the water after 10 minutes and again after 20 minutes. If using immediately, use a wide, shallow spoon (held just under the surface) to remove the liquid fat, or use a fat separator. Otherwise, cover and refrigerate overnight.

The next day, lift and scrape the congealed fat from the surface using a slotted spoon or a large serving spoon. Store, covered, in the refrigerator for up to 3 days. To keep longer, freeze in a container, allowing 1-inch of headspace, for up to 6 months.

Makes 3 to 6 quarts.

COOK'S NOTE   *Start today to develop a very smart habit: Store chicken necks, tails, wing tips, gizzards, hearts, backs, rib (breast) bones—anything except livers—in a gallon-size lock-top freezer bag in your freezer. When the bag is full, you have enough chicken parts to make a small pot of homemade stock. Squeeze the excess air out of the bag each time you add chicken pieces; this helps to prevent the dehydration known as freezer burn.*

Linguine with Broccoli and Blue Cheese

Serves 4

This recipe uses only a few ingredients, takes only little time, and makes an appealing pasta dish. For a meal that's even faster to prepare, use fresh linguine.

½ recipe Steamed Broccoli (page 19)
1 tablespoon salt
1 cup Chicken Stock (page 23) or canned low-salt chicken broth
½ cup finely diced yellow onion
1 cup heavy (whipping) cream
8 ounces blue cheese, crumbled or coarsely chopped
½ teaspoon hot pepper sauce
½ teaspoon ground nutmeg
1 pound dried linguine
1 cup lightly packed fresh parsley leaves, coarsely chopped

Trim the broccoli into bite-sized florets and bring it to room temperature. In a 7-quart or larger pot, bring 6 quarts water to a boil, then add the salt. Lower the heat to a simmer and cover while you make the sauce.

In a 2-quart saucepan, bring the stock or broth and onion to a boil over medium-high heat. Cook until reduced by half, about 5 minutes. Lower heat to medium and add the cream, blue cheese, hot pepper sauce, and nutmeg. Cook until the cheese is melted. Cover and keep warm while you cook the pasta.

Return the pasta water to a full boil. Add the linguine, stir, and cook until al dente (cooked through but still slightly chewy), about 8 minutes. About 1 minute before the linguine is done, put the broccoli in the pan with the sauce to warm. Drain the noodles and return them to the pan. Add the parsley and the sauce mixture, and toss. Divide among 4 warmed soup plates or pasta bowls. Serve.

Asian Chicken Salad with Green Onion–Sesame Dressing

Serves 4

This is a refreshing, not-too-assertive cabbage and cellophane noodle–based salad. Cellophane noodles (also known as Chinese vermicelli and bean threads) are thin, opaque noodles sold in dried bundles. When soaked they become translucent. They have little taste of their own, but soak up the delicious flavors of the dressing.

DRESSING:

1 tablespoon soy sauce
1 tablespoon rice vinegar
½ teaspoon granulated sugar
2 teaspoons Asian sesame oil
¼ cup vegetable oil
½ cup raw sesame seeds

2 tablespoons vegetable oil
3 green onions
2 quarter-size slices unpeeled fresh ginger
2 large garlic cloves
½ head green cabbage (about 1 pound)
2 bunches cellophane noodles (1¾ ounces each), soaked in hot water 15 minutes, drained, and quartered like a pizza
1 large carrot
½ large cucumber (about 6 ounces)
1 cup lightly packed fresh cilantro, minced
½ Roast Chicken with Lemon, Garlic, and Fresh Rosemary (page 17), skinned, boned, and shredded
Freshly ground pepper to taste

TO MAKE THE DRESSING: Combine the soy sauce, rice vinegar, sugar, sesame oil, and vegetable oil in a small bowl and whisk together. Put the sesame seeds in a small dry skillet over medium heat. Toast, stirring, until lightly browned but not burned. Scrape the seeds into the dressing.

Thinly slice the white and light green parts of the green onions, and mince the green tops. Mince the ginger and garlic, and shred the cabbage. Peel and shred the carrot, and peel, quarter lengthwise, seed, and thinly slice the cucumber. Mince the cilantro.

In a 12-inch sauté pan or skillet over medium heat, heat the oil and sauté the white and light green parts of the green onions, the ginger, and garlic for about 30 seconds. Add the cabbage, tossing and stirring to brighten its color and wilt it slightly, about 2 minutes. Add the cellophane noodles, toss well, and turn out into a large bowl. Add the remaining ingredients. Toss, add the dressing, toss again, and serve.

weekend

PEPPER-CRUSTED TUNA STEAKS
GRILLED ASPARAGUS
GRILLED BABY POTATOES
STRAWBERRY SHORTCAKES

monday

NIÇOISE SALAD
The leftover tuna is used instead of canned tuna for a classic salad. The extra shortcakes are served again with strawberries, or with any other fragrant berry the market has to offer.

wednesday

SKILLET SCRAMBLE OF GRILLED POTATOES AND ASPARAGUS
Leftover grilled potatoes are combined with eggs, colorful red peppers, and savory onion for a quick supper dish. Variations on this recipe are limited only by your imagination.

thursday

PASTA WITH GRILLED ASPARAGUS, PINE NUTS, AND OLIVE OIL
The extra grilled asparagus is used in a delicious and simple vegetarian pasta dish punctuated with toasty pine nuts and olive oil.

Ahi tuna is a meat-lover's fish. It is firm, rich, and full of flavor. In this menu, we enhance its meaty character by coating the steaks in a black olive tapenade and pressing in coarsely crushed black peppercorns.

The rest of this weekend meal is a breeze: grilled asparagus and lots of grilled new potatoes tossed with olive oil and parsley. The meal is finished with one of the most popular American desserts, strawberry shortcakes.

The morning of serving, or several hours in advance, make the shortcakes. Two to three hours before dinner, prepare the strawberries, toss with sugar, and leave at room temperature. While the grill is heating, prepare the tuna and asparagus. Grill the potatoes first and keep them warm while cooking the tuna and asparagus.

Ahi is not inexpensive, but cooking some extra will provide a fabulous salad a day or so later. Plenty of grilled vegetables are the basis for two other quick weeknight meals.

Pepper-Crusted Tuna Steaks

Serves 4, with 2 steaks reserved for Niçoise Salad (page 34)

You don't need an ingredient list a mile long to create glorious food. Quality ingredients, simply prepared, is the secret here. The inspiration for this dish was a casual bistro lunch in Paris of steak au poivre and frites.

3 tablespoons extra-virgin olive oil

½ cup black olive tapenade (see Cook's Notes)

3 tablespoons kosher salt

½ cup coarsely crushed peppercorns (see Cook's Notes)

6 ahi tuna steaks, about 6 ounces each and 1 to 1¼ inches thick

4 lemon wedges

In a small bowl, combine the olive oil and tapenade. Mix to blend. Set aside at room temperature until ready to serve.

Light a hot fire in a charcoal grill or preheat a gas or electric grill. Oil the cooking rack. Mix the salt and crushed peppercorns together and spread the mixture out on a dinner plate. Press each tuna steak into the salt mixture until heavily coated on both sides. Set aside on a plate or platter.

Put the tuna on the cooking rack. Cover the grill and cook the steaks on one side for 3 minutes. Turn and cook the second side for about 3 minutes, or until an instant-read thermometer registers 120°F when inserted into the center of a steak.

Spoon 2 tablespoons of the olive sauce over each steak. Serve 4 steaks immediately with a lemon wedge on each plate. Reserve 2 steaks for the Niçoise Salad (page 34). Let them cool, wrap them well, and store in the refrigerator for up to 3 days.

COOK'S NOTES *Tapenade is a coarsely crushed olive mixture used in Mediterranean cooking. It is easy to make your own, but for this recipe we suggest buying prepared tapenade. Look for it in the specialty foods section of a supermarket or other specialty foods stores carrying Italian and Mediterranean ingredients. Once the jar is opened, it will keep for several months stored in the refrigerator.*

Some pepper mills allow you to adjust the grind from fine to coarse. If you don't have one, place whole peppercorns in a sealed heavy plastic bag and use a rolling pin or a heavy pan to coarsely crush the peppercorns.

This recipe works equally well as a sauté: Heat a heavy skillet, preferably cast iron, until hot but not smoking. Add 2 tablespoons olive oil, swirl the pan to coat it, and add the tuna steaks. Follow the same timing as the grill method.

Grilled Asparagus

Serves 4, with 15 spears reserved for Pasta with Grilled Asparagus, Pine Nuts, and Olive Oil (page 37), and 8 spears reserved for Skillet Scramble of Grilled Potatoes and Asparagus (page 35)

While you grill the tuna—or just before—pop the asparagus spears on the grill. You will be rewarded in this meal as well as in a pasta meal a few days later.

43 thick asparagus spears
2 tablespoons olive oil
   Salt and freshly ground pepper to taste

Prepare the grill with a hot fire. Snap off the fibrous bottom end of each spear or trim the whole bunch with a knife to a uniform length. Peel the spears from slightly below the tip to the base, using a sharp vegetable peeler or paring knife. In a large bowl or baking dish, toss the asparagus with the oil, salt, and pepper.

Lay the spears on the grill over a hot fire. Cover, cook for 3 minutes, then turn. Cover and cook for 3 minutes more, or until crisp-tender. If you are not grilling, steam or boil the asparagus until crisp-tender. Serve 5 spears to each diner. Cool, wrap, and refrigerate the remainder.

Grilled Baby Potatoes

Serves 4, with 12 potatoes reserved for Skillet Scramble of Grilled Potatoes and Asparagus (page 35)

Grilling potatoes is ridiculously easy and lends a smoky flavor to the little tubers that is unlike anything else. What you don't eat at one sitting becomes leftovers for salads, hashes, scrambles, and meals of all kinds. If you don't want to grill them, see Cook's Note.

3⅓ pounds unpeeled baby red or white
  potatoes (about 32)
3 tablespoons olive oil
  Scant ¼ teaspoon salt
  Dusting of freshly ground pepper

Prepare the grill with a hot fire. In a medium bowl, toss the potatoes with the oil, salt, and pepper. Place them on the grill, cover, and cook for about 10 minutes. Turn, cover, and cook for about 10 minutes more, until easily pierced with a knife.

Set aside 12 potatoes to cool and serve the rest. Wrap and refrigerate the reserved potatoes.

COOK'S NOTE *To bake the potatoes instead of grilling them, spread them in a shallow baking dish and bake for about 35 minutes in a preheated 350°F oven.*

Strawberry Shortcakes

Serves 4, with 4 shortcakes reserved for a second dessert

The words strawberry shortcake *evoke warm smiles and deep sighs. Everybody loves this truly American dessert. Our version was inspired by a James Beard recipe for cream biscuits. You'll have enough of these delicious biscuits for another shortcake dessert later in the week.*

2 cups (1 pint) fresh strawberries, hulled
1 tablespoon granulated sugar

Cut the berries in half, or in quarters if they are large. Place them in a medium bowl and toss with the sugar. (The berries are best if tossed with sugar at least 1 hour before serving to release some juices. They can be prepared several hours in advance, refrigerated, and then removed from refrigerator 1 hour before serving.)

SHORTCAKES:

2 cups all-purpose flour
1 tablespoon baking powder
¼ teaspoon salt
¼ cup granulated sugar
4 tablespoons (½ stick) cold unsalted butter, cut into 8 pieces
1 large egg
⅓ cup heavy (whipping) cream

TO MAKE THE SHORTCAKES: Preheat the oven to 450°F. Place the flour, baking powder, salt, and sugar in a large bowl. Work the butter into the flour with your fingertips or a pastry cutter until the mixture is the texture of coarse meal. In a small bowl, mix the egg with the cream. Pour this into the flour mixture, blending with a table fork until the mixture is moistened and the liquid absorbed. Turn the dough out onto a floured work surface. Knead a few times, just enough to hold the dough together. If the dough is too crumbly to hold together, add drops of water a few at a time until the dough will hold together. Pat the dough into a circle ½ to ¾ inch thick. Using a 2½-inch biscuit cutter or the top of a drinking glass, cut out biscuits. Place them on an ungreased baking sheet. Bake until nicely browned, 12 to 14 minutes.

TOPPING:

1 cup (½ pint) cold heavy (whipping)
 cream
1 tablespoon granulated sugar

TO MAKE THE TOPPING: Combine the cream and sugar in a deep bowl. Beat with chilled beaters until soft peaks form. To serve, split 4 warm biscuits in half. Divide the strawberries among the bottom halves and place the tops on. Top each shortcake with a generous dollop of whipped cream and serve immediately before they get soggy. Cool, wrap, and freeze the leftover biscuits.

COOK'S NOTES *Rewarm frozen biscuits in a preheated 300°F oven for 15 minutes. You can make mixed-berry shortcakes by mixing 2 cups of any combination of blueberries, raspberries, blackberries, and so on. Toss them with 1 tablespoon sugar, or to taste, and proceed to assemble the shortcakes as above.*

These biscuits are also wonderful with jam or honey for breakfast.

Niçoise Salad

Serves 4

There are few better uses for leftover cooked tuna than this classic salad, always a crowd-pleaser. Create individual servings or prepare one impressive large platter or bowl.

4 unpeeled small potatoes (about 12 ounces)
12 ounces green beans, trimmed
   Leaves from 1 head romaine lettuce
2 hard-cooked eggs, shelled, each cut into 8 slices or wedges
3 medium tomatoes (about 1 pound), each cut into 8 wedges
8 cured black or green olives, pitted and sliced
2 Pepper-Crusted Tuna Steaks (page 29), cut into ¼-inch slices (about 2½ cups)
½ cup minced fresh parsley

Boil or steam the potatoes until they are barely tender when pierced with a knife, about 20 to 25 minutes. Drain, let cool, and cut each into 8 wedges. Trim the beans and boil or steam them until they are just tender, about 5 to 7 minutes. Drain, put them in ice water for 5 minutes, drain again, and dry on paper towels.

Arrange the salad any way you like on individual plates or on one large platter or bowl. You can arrange piles or rows of each ingredient side by side on top of a bed of torn or cut romaine, or toss all the ingredients except the lettuce together and arrange them on the romaine leaves. Or, tear the romaine into pieces and toss them with the salad.

DRESSING:
½ cup extra-virgin olive oil
3 tablespoons fresh lemon juice
1 teaspoon anchovy paste
2 teaspoons Dijon-style mustard
½ teaspoon salt
   Freshly ground pepper to taste

TO MAKE THE DRESSING: Whisk together all the dressing ingredients. Pour over a composed salad or toss with a tossed salad.

Skillet Scramble of Grilled Potatoes and Asparagus

Serves 4

Omelets are an elegant way to make use of leftover foods. A scramble is a simpler way to do the same thing. There aren't many meals that are as quick and tasty. Serve with a good loaf of crusty bread.

4 tablespoons (½ stick) unsalted butter

1 red bell pepper (about 6 ounces), seeded, deribbed, and cut into ½-inch dice

1 small red onion (3 to 4 ounces), cut into ¼-inch dice

12 Grilled Baby Potatoes (page 31), quartered

8 spears Grilled Asparagus (page 30)

¼ cup fresh thyme leaves, minced

12 large eggs

½ teaspoon hot pepper sauce

¼ teaspoon salt

In a 12-inch nonstick skillet, melt the butter over medium heat and sauté the pepper and onion until soft but not browned, about 5 minutes. Add the potatoes, asparagus, and thyme leaves. Cook, stirring occasionally, until the potatoes are warm in the center (try one), about 5 minutes.

In a medium bowl, beat the eggs, hot pepper sauce, and salt together just until blended. Pour them into the pan and cook, stirring almost constantly, until the eggs are softly set. Serve at once on gently warmed plates.

Pasta with Grilled Asparagus, Pine Nuts, and Olive Oil

Serves 4

This pasta dish is the perfect vehicle for leftover asparagus. You'll have dinner made in the time it takes to boil water and cook the pasta.

½ cup (2½ ounces) pine nuts
1 tablespoon plus ½ teaspoon salt
1 pound dried bow tie (farfalle) pasta
15 spears Grilled Asparagus (page 30), cut into 1-inch lengths
⅓ cup extra-virgin olive oil
⅓ cup minced fresh parsley
Freshly ground pepper to taste
½ cup (2 ounces) grated Parmesan cheese

Fill an 8- to 10-quart stockpot two-thirds full of water, cover, and bring to a boil over high heat. Heat a dry 8-inch skillet over medium-high heat. When hot, but not smoking, add the pine nuts and toast them, stirring constantly, until lightly browned, about 3 minutes. Pour out onto a small plate to cool.

When the pasta water has reached a boil, add the 1 tablespoon salt. Add the pasta, stir, and cook until al dente (cooked through but still slightly chewy). Drain thoroughly in a colander, leaving about ¼ cup cooking water in the bottom of the stockpot to use in the sauce.

Return the pasta to the pot with the reserved cooking water. Add the pine nuts, asparagus, olive oil, parsley, ½ teaspoon salt, and pepper to taste. Toss well and divide among individual plates or bowls. Serve immediately, with the Parmesan alongside to be sprinkled on the pasta.

monday

PORK AND CHEDDAR SUBS
Thinly sliced pork roast combined with a
good-quality Cheddar cheese makes an
excellent sandwich on a warm baguette.
A simple mustard-yogurt-mayonnaise
spread completes the picture.

wednesday

FRIED RICE WITH JULIENNED PORK
The remaining pilaf becomes fried rice,
with pork (this time finely julienned), egg,
and vegetables.

thursday

**BEEF BARLEY SOUP
WITH ROASTED VEGETABLES**
Delicious leftover roasted vegetables are
rediscovered in a stick-to-your-ribs soup
that includes some ground beef or lamb,
beef broth, and pearl barley.

Even though this menu is scheduled for weekend preparation, the meat cookery is quick and simple. In addition to the tasty pork, the main meal includes an aromatic rice pilaf, a caramelized mélange of roasted vegetables, and an absolutely indulgent dessert, Mocha Pôts de Crème.

The pôts de crème must be made at least 6 hours in advance, or the day before serving. The dry rub for the pork can be made early in the day of cooking. Everything else comes together quickly. Start by roasting the vegetables. Then make the pilaf. Rub the pork with the spice mixture, brown in a skillet, and then pop in the oven for about five minutes (yes, that is correct, five minutes) as the roasted vegetables come out. Cover the vegetables with aluminum foil to keep them warm.

This dinner parlays into three more fine ones for the coming week: a great sandwich, comfy fried rice, and a hearty soup.

Roast Pork Tenderloin

Makes 2 tenderloins, 1 to serve (for 4 people) and 1 reserved for the Pork and Cheddar Subs (page 47) and Fried Rice with Julienned Pork (page 48)

The combination of a dry rub and roasting at high heat provides a flavorful entrée with very little effort. The rubs can be varied according to what is in the spice cupboard.

2 pork tenderloins (about 2 pounds total)	Preheat the oven to 450°F. Thoroughly dry the tenderloins with paper towels. Remove the thin silverskin membrane, if necessary, by inserting a sharp boning knife under it and cutting it away, keeping the knife angled slightly toward the silverskin.

DRY RUB:

2 teaspoons cumin seed
1 teaspoon ground ginger
1 tablespoon paprika
1 tablespoon packed brown sugar
1 teaspoon ground pepper
1 tablespoon dried thyme

2 tablespoons vegetable oil

TO MAKE THE RUB: In a dry heavy skillet over medium heat, toast the cumin, stirring often, until it is fragrant, about 5 minutes. Remove from the pan and cool thoroughly. Grind the cumin in a spice grinder or with a mortar and pestle. Combine the ground cumin with the remaining ingredients. With your hands, spread the dry rub all over both tenderloins.

Heat a 12-inch heavy ovenproof skillet over medium-high heat until quite hot. Add the vegetable oil and immediately add the tenderloins, being careful to avoid splatters. Cook until very well browned on one side, about 5 minutes. Turn the tenderloins and immediately place the skillet in the preheated oven. Roast for 5 minutes. Remove the pan from the oven and test the meat's temperature with an instant-read thermometer. It should read 145°F. If it does not, place the pan (but not the thermometer) back in the oven for another minute or two, then check the temperature again. Transfer the tenderloins to a carving board and let rest for 5 minutes. Cut 1 tenderloin into ¼-inch slices and serve on warm plates. Cool, wrap, and refrigerate the other tenderloin.

COOK'S NOTE *The dry rub can be made a couple of days in advance and kept in jar at a cool room temperature.*

Red Pepper Rice Pilaf

Serves 4, with 6 cups reserved for Fried Rice with Julienned Pork (page 48)

To make a pilaf, dry rice is stirred in a hot pan along with a little oil or butter (and other seasonings, if desired) until the grains become opaque. Then cooking liquid is added and the rice is steamed. The result is a dish of separate, glistening grains. It is easy to turn leftovers into fried rice.

3 tablespoons vegetable oil

1 red bell pepper (about 6 ounces), seeded, deribbed, and cut into ¼-inch dice

1 small (about 2 ounces) onion, cut into ¼-inch dice

3 cups long-grain white rice, preferably basmati

4½ cups water

2½ teaspoons salt

Freshly ground pepper to taste

1 small bay leaf, broken in two

1½ teaspoons celery seed

In a 4-quart or larger heavy saucepan over medium heat, heat the oil and sauté the pepper and onion until they are slightly softened but not browned, about 2 minutes. Add the rice and stir until opaque, 3 to 5 minutes. Add the water, salt, pepper, bay leaf, and celery seed. Stir, bring the water to a boil, reduce to a bare simmer, cover, and cook for 15 minutes. Remove from heat and let sit for 5 to 15 minutes. Stir the pilaf and remove the bay leaves.

Reserve 6 cups of the rice and serve the rest. Cool the reserved rice, cover, and refrigerate for up to 7 days.

Roasted Carrot, Rutabaga, and Turnip Mélange

Serves 4, with 4 cups reserved for Beef Barley Soup with Roasted Vegetables (page 49)

Roasting is one of the easiest methods of cooking root vegetables. Since a hot oven is necessary to cook the pork tenderloin, the vegetables may be roasted just in advance of the meat. After roasting, cover the vegetables with aluminum foil to keep them warm while the pork is roasted.

4 pounds mixed carrots, rutabagas, and
   turnips, peeled and cut into 1- to
   1½-inch cubes
2 tablespoons vegetable oil
2 teaspoons salt
   Freshly ground pepper to taste

Preheat the oven to 425°F. Line a heavy baking pan with aluminum foil to make cleanup easier, or choose a nonstick pan. In a large bowl, toss the vegetables with the oil, salt, and pepper to mix well. Spread the vegetables in a single layer on the baking sheet. Roast until a cake tester or toothpick slides easily into a vegetable cube, about 45 minutes.

Set aside 4 cups of the vegetables to cool and serve the rest. Wrap and refrigerate the reserved vegetables for up to 7 days.

Mocha Pôts de Crème

Serves 4, with 4 reserved for a weeknight dessert

Wait until you taste this dessert! The luscious flavors of chocolate, coffee, and cinnamon marry in a delightfully rich custard. Use the classic white six-ounce ramekins for these pôts de crème, or for fun, use small porcelain coffee mugs. With a dollop of whipped cream for garnish, it looks like hot chocolate.

1½ cups milk

1½ cups heavy (whipping) cream

½ cup espresso coffee beans, lightly crushed (see Cook's Notes, page 46)

3 tablespoons granulated sugar

1 cinnamon stick, or ¼ teaspoon ground cinnamon

5 ounces semisweet baking chocolate, chopped into small pieces

4 large egg yolks

2 large eggs

In a heavy 2-quart saucepan, combine the milk, cream, coffee beans, sugar, cinnamon, and chocolate. Cook over medium heat, stirring frequently, until the chocolate is melted and the sugar is dissolved, about 10 minutes. The mixture should remain just below a simmer. Remove from heat and let cool for 25 minutes.

Preheat the oven to 350°F. Have ready eight 4-ounce ramekins and two 9-by-13-inch baking dishes. In a medium bowl, whisk the egg yolks and eggs until well beaten. Pour the cooled milk mixture into the eggs and stir until completely blended. Use a rubber spatula to scrape any remaining bits of chocolate or coffee from the saucepan. Place a fine-meshed sieve over the saucepan and pour the milk mixture back into the saucepan.

Divide the mixture among the ramekins. Set 4 ramekins in each baking dish and set the baking dishes on the center rack of oven. Pour warm—not hot—water into the baking dishes until water comes about two-thirds of the way up the sides of the ramekins. Cover loosely with aluminum foil and bake until the custards are just set in the center, 40 to 45 minutes. Remove from the water bath and let cool on wire racks for 30 minutes, then cover and refrigerate for at least 6 hours or overnight.

continued on page 46

GARNISH:

½ cup heavy (whipping) cream

2 teaspoons powdered sugar, sifted

Just before serving, make the garnish: In a deep bowl, beat the cream and powdered sugar until soft peaks form. Leave 4 of the pôts de crème refrigerated, ungarnished, for a weeknight dessert. Top the other 4 with a dollop of whipped cream and serve.

COOK'S NOTES *The easiest way to crush coffee beans is to place them in a heavy lock-top plastic bag. Use a rolling pin or a heavy pot to crush the beans.*

The reserved pôts de crème will keep well in the refrigerator for 3 to 4 days.

Leftover whipped cream can be covered with plastic wrap and refrigerated for up to 2 days. As the whipped cream sits, some liquid will separate to the bottom; don't try to mix it together, just use the thickened cream on top.

Pork and Cheddar Subs

Serves 4

In almost the time it takes to get through the drive-up line at your local fast-food emporium, you can put together a knock-out sandwich using leftover roast pork tenderloin. Serve it with fresh-pack (refrigerated) dill pickles and a bowlful of your favorite thick-sliced potato chips.

1 pound crusty baguettes	Warm the baguette(s) in a 150°F oven.

DRESSING:

¼ cup mayonnaise

2 tablespoons plain yogurt

1½ tablespoons Dijon-style mustard

6 dried apricot halves, finely chopped

¼ teaspoon salt

Freshly ground pepper to taste

¾ of 1 Roast Pork Tenderloin (page 41), very thinly sliced

4 ounces medium-sharp Cheddar cheese, thinly sliced

A few very thin slices yellow onion

6–8 fresh arugula leaves or other young bitter greens

TO MAKE THE DRESSING: Mix all the dressing ingredients together in medium bowl.

Remove the baguette(s) from the oven and slice in half lengthwise. Spread the cut sides of both slices with dressing. Place the onion slices on the bottom piece of bread. Top with the sliced meat and cheese. Place the arugula leaves on top of the cheese and top with the other baguette half. Press down firmly. Cut into 4 sandwiches with a serrated bread knife. Serve.

Fried Rice with Julienned Pork

Serves 4

This recipe is one of our top-ten frequently made weeknight dishes. Ten minutes of chopping, ten minutes of cooking, and dinner is on the table.

2 tablespoons vegetable oil

2 large eggs, beaten

2 medium carrots, peeled and cut into ⅛-inch-thick diagonal slices

2 ribs celery, tops removed, cut into ¼-inch-thick diagonal slices

2 tablespoons dry sherry

6 cups Red Pepper Rice Pilaf (page 42)

¼ of 1 Roast Pork Tenderloin (page 41), cut into julienne

2 green onions, including green tops, cut into ¼-inch-thick diagonal slices

2 teaspoons low-salt soy sauce

1 tablespoon Asian sesame oil

Heat a 14-inch wok or 12-inch skillet over high heat until hot, about 1 minute. Add 1 tablespoon of the vegetable oil; swirl it around the pan and pour in the eggs. Allow them to set for about 15 seconds, then begin to stir with a spatula. Cook until the eggs are scrambled to a medium-soft custardy stage. Set aside on a plate.

Add the remaining 1 tablespoon oil to the pan, swirl, and heat over high heat until it just begins to smoke. Add the carrots and celery. Stir-fry for 3 to 4 minutes, or until vegetables are crisp-tender. Add the sherry and stir-fry until absorbed. Add the rice and stir-fry until hot, about 3 minutes. Add the pork and green onions; stir-fry for 1 minute. Add the soy sauce and sesame oil, stir to combine, then return the eggs to the pan. Stir-fry for 30 seconds to thoroughly combine, then remove to a heated serving bowl or plates. Serve immediately.

Beef Barley Soup with Roasted Vegetables

Serves 4

This is hearty, stick-to-your-ribs fare. Lamb can be substituted for the beef. Take some to work for lunch if your workplace has a microwave.

4 cups Roasted Carrot, Rutabaga, and Turnip Mélange (page 43)
2 tablespoons vegetable oil
1 large yellow onion (10 to 12 ounces), cut into ½-inch dice or coarsely chopped
1 large garlic clove, minced
½ pound very lean ground beef or lamb
2 ribs celery, cut into ¼-inch dice
2 cans (14½ ounces *each*) low-salt beef broth
1 can (14½ ounces) diced tomatoes with juice
2 cups milk
1 cup pearl barley
1 small bay leaf
1½ teaspoons dried thyme
Freshly ground pepper to taste

Cut the roasted vegetables into ½-inch pieces and let sit at room temperature.

In a 4-quart heavy saucepan over medium heat, heat the oil and sauté the onion and garlic until softened but not browned, about 5 minutes. Add the ground beef or lamb and sauté, breaking up the lumps, until the meat has lost its pink color. Add all the remaining ingredients except the roasted vegetables. Bring almost to a boil, reduce to a simmer, cover, and cook until barley is tender, about 30 minutes. Place the room-temperature roasted vegetables in warmed soup bowls and ladle the soup into the bowls. Serve.

weekend

ROAST DUCK WITH BALSAMIC GLAZE
POLENTA WITH GORGONZOLA SAUCE
BRAISED FENNEL AND ONION WITH TARRAGON
APPLE-CURRANT TART

monday

**SAUTÉED POLENTA SQUARES
WITH ITALIAN SAUSAGE SAUCE**
The reserved polenta is cut into squares and sautéed until golden, then topped with a quick Italian sausage and tomato sauce. This is a filling and delicious weeknight supper.

wednesday

PASTA WITH FENNEL, ENDIVE, AND WALNUTS
Leftover braised fennel becomes the basis for a vegetarian pasta dish accented with toasted walnuts.

thursday

ROAST DUCK SOFT TACOS
This easy and fun meal, where everyone assembles his or her own tacos, combines tender roast duck and roasted red peppers.

A simple roast duck makes an elegant weekend meal. If you use frozen ducks, you will need 2 to 3 days to defrost them in the refrigerator. The elegant nature of this menu continues with two slightly unusual accompaniments: soft, luscious polenta with Gorgonzola sauce, and braised fennel. A gorgeous, just-baked apple-currant tart makes a beautiful finish.

The tart crust should be made the morning of serving to allow time to chill. It can also be made several days in advance and frozen. Thaw it gently overnight in the refrigerator. The tart can be filled and baked several hours before serving and left at room temperature. While the duck is roasting, braise the fennel. It can be kept warm for thirty minutes. Melt the Gorgonzola sauce and begin cooking the polenta about twenty-five minutes before the duck is due out of oven.

This lovely meal will provide for 3 more casual ones during the week: tacos, pasta, and some polenta squares.

Roast Duck with Balsamic Glaze

Serves 4, with ½ duck reserved for Roast Duck Soft Tacos (page 61)

Our recipe in The Basic Gourmet *for Roast Duck with Apple-Onion Sauté uses the technique of browning the ducks first, then roasting them, then finishing them under the broiler to produce a crisp skin. This recipe is even easier, skipping the browning step. Balsamic vinegar, reduced to a syrup and brushed on the ducks during their last fifteen minutes of cooking, gives the skin a marvelously sweet-tart flavor. You'll need two ducks to serve four, saving at least half of a duck to make duck tacos another day. Enjoy the livers sautéed, thinly sliced, and added to a salad. Save the giblets and necks for making stock.*

2 ducklings, about 5 pounds each, thawed if frozen
Salt and freshly ground pepper to taste
1⅓ cups balsamic vinegar

Preheat the oven to 350°F. Select a roasting pan with sides at least 1 inch high, with a rack on which both ducks will fit, or roast them separately. Remove the necks and giblets from the ducks. Dry the ducks with paper towels, sprinkle with salt and pepper, and place in the pan. Roast the ducks for 1¾ hours.

Meanwhile, in a nonreactive 1-quart saucepan boil the vinegar over medium-high heat until it has reduced to a syrup that can be brushed on the ducks. Watch carefully; don't let it boil dry.

Remove the ducks from the oven, brush all over with the balsamic syrup, and return to the oven for 15 more minutes. Remove the ducks from the oven, preheat the broiler, and finish the ducks by broiling them on both sides until a very dark brown. Let rest for 5 minutes, then carve 1½ ducks and serve, setting the remaining ½ duck aside to cool completely.

Remove the skin and bones from the reserved ½ duck, and cut the meat into ¼-inch pieces. Wrap and refrigerate for up to 5 days.

Polenta with Gorgonzola Sauce

Serves 4 (½ cup each), with the rest reserved for Sautéed Polenta Squares (page 59)

Polenta is Italian-style cornmeal mush, and is it good! Top it with a creamy Gorgonzola (Italian blue cheese) sauce and enjoy a special taste treat. The polenta that is not served soft with the sauce is spread in an oiled pan to become the basis for sautéed polenta squares later in the week. Look for polenta (coarsely ground cornmeal) in the supermarket where specialty flours are sold. Gorgonzola is delicious, but if not available, substitute another blue cheese such as Maytag or Oregon Blue.

---

2 quarts water
1 teaspoon salt, plus salt to taste
3 cups polenta
 Freshly ground pepper to taste

In a 4-quart heavy saucepan bring the water to a boil over medium-high heat. Add the 1 teaspoon salt. Pour the polenta into the boiling water in a steady stream, stirring briskly with a wooden spoon. Reduce heat to maintain a very slow boil. Be careful it does not boil too quickly, or it can spatter and burn the cook. Stir frequently until the polenta pulls away from the sides of the pan and a wooden spoon will stand upright in it, 20 to 30 minutes. Add pepper and more salt, if desired.

SAUCE:

4 ounces Gorgonzola cheese
¼ cup milk
¼ cup heavy (whipping) cream
½ teaspoon salt

TO MAKE THE SAUCE: While the polenta cooks combine the cheese, milk, and cream in a 1-quart saucepan. Warm over very low heat until the cheese is melted and the sauce has thickened slightly. Add the salt and stir.

When ready to serve, oil a 10-by-15-inch jelly roll pan and place it near the polenta. Place ½ cup soft polenta on each of 4 warm dinner plates. Make a well in the center of each mound with the back of a spoon. Place the plates back in a warm oven for a couple of minutes while you spoon the rest of polenta out into the prepared pan. Spread the polenta out with wet hands until it is a rectangular shape about ½ inch thick. Do not worry if it does not fill the pan. Let cool, cover with plastic wrap, and refrigerate.

Take the plates from the oven and pour Gorgonzola sauce into the wells in each mound of polenta. Serve immediately.

Braised Fennel and Onion with Tarragon

Serves 4, with 2 cups reserved for Pasta with Fennel, Endive, and Walnuts (page 60)

Fennel, also often labeled as sweet anise, is available in many supermarkets and specialty produce stores. The bulb, when sliced, separates much like an onion. The fernlike top is sometimes chopped and used as a seasoning. Fennel has a very mild licorice flavor, and in this case provides a nice foil for the richness of the duck and the Gorgonzola sauce.

2 tablespoons olive oil

1 small to medium yellow onion (5 to 6 ounces), halved, and cut into ¼-inch slices

3 fennel bulbs, trimmed of stalks, halved, and cut into ¼-inch slices

½ cup Chicken Stock (page 23), or canned low-salt chicken broth

¼ cup lightly packed fresh tarragon leaves, chopped, or 1½ teaspoons dried tarragon

Salt and freshly ground pepper to taste

In a 12-inch sauté pan or skillet over medium-high heat, heat the oil and add the onion and fennel. Toss to blend, then add the stock or broth, tarragon, and pepper. Cover and cook over medium to medium-low heat until the fennel is crisp-tender, 10 to 15 minutes. Remove the lid, raise heat to medium-high, and boil away all but a few tablespoons of the juices. Add salt. Set 2 cups aside to cool.

Serve the rest immediately. Wrap, and refrigerate the reserved fennel for up to 5 days.

Apple-Currant Tart

Serves 4, with 4 slices reserved for the following night's dessert

---

Tarts are easier to make than pies, because you don't have crimped edges to worry about. Two-piece metal tart pans typically have a scalloped edge. Once the pastry dough is fitted into the pan, all that is required is a sweep across the top with a rolling pin, and voilà—you have a lovely scalloped edge of dough.

CRUST:

2½ cups all-purpose flour

1 teaspoon salt

3 tablespoons granulated sugar

½ cup (1 stick) plus 3 tablespoons cold
   unsalted butter, cut into small pieces

7 tablespoons cold solid vegetable shortening

2 tablespoons heavy (whipping) cream

2 teaspoons pure vanilla extract

2 tablespoons ice water, plus more if
   needed

TO MAKE THE CRUST: Put the dry ingredients in a food processor and pulse to blend. Add the butter and shortening and pulse just until the mixture resembles coarse crumbs. Add the cream, vanilla, and 2 tablespoons ice water. Process for a few seconds, just until a ball of dough begins to form. Add more water 1 table-spoon at a time if needed to form the dough into a mass; do not process after the dough ball forms. (To make the dough by hand, use two knives or a pastry blade to cut the butter and shortening into the dry ingredients, and a fork or your fingers to mix in the liquids and gently form a mass.) Remove the dough, gathering all loose bits, and divide into 2 equal pieces.

Form each piece of dough into a ball, flatten to about 1 inch thick, and enclose in plastic wrap. Refrigerate one piece for at least 30 minutes or up to overnight. Double wrap the second piece, label and date it, and freeze to make a tart on another weekend. When ready to use, defrost in the refrigerator.

FILLING:

¼ cup fresh orange juice

¾ cup packed brown sugar

¼ cup dried currants

4 crisp apples (1¼ to 1½ pounds), such as
Gala or Yellow Delicious, peeled, cored,
and cut into ¼-inch-thick slices

½ teaspoon ground cinnamon

1½ tablespoons all-purpose flour

3 tablespoons orange marmalade

1 pint vanilla ice cream, or ¾ cup heavy
(whipping) cream and 2 tablespoons
powdered sugar, whipped until soft
peaks form (optional)

TO MAKE THE FILLING: In a large bowl, combine the orange juice, brown sugar, and currants. Add the apples and toss to combine. Add the cinnamon and flour, then stir to combine. Let sit while you roll out the dough.

On a lightly floured work surface, roll the dough out to a circle about 12 inches in diameter. Dust the work surface and dough with a little more flour if necessary to keep the dough from sticking. The dough will be very delicate, and its edges will not be perfectly smooth. Roll the dough circle around the rolling pin, lift it over one side of a 9- or 10-inch tart pan with a removable bottom, and unroll the dough over the pan, allowing it to settle into place. Using your fingers, lightly press the dough into the sides of the pan. Fold over the extra overhanging dough to evenly double the side walls of the tart. If some places have no overhanging dough, patch some in. With a light touch, run the rolling pin across the top of the tart, cutting off the excess dough. Put the tart in the freezer for 20 minutes.

Preheat the oven to 400°F. Position a rack in the center of the oven. Arrange the apple slices in overlapping concentric circles in the tart shell, starting from the outside edge and working towards the middle. Pour any remaining liquid over the apples, evenly distributing the currants.

Bake for 35 to 40 minutes, or until the crust is nicely browned and the apples are tender when pierced with a knife. Turn the oven temperature to 450°F, brush the tart with marmalade, and bake for 5 minutes, or until the glaze is melted and bubbly. Let cool on a wire rack for at least 1 hour.

Cut the tart into eighths. Set 4 slices aside, cover loosely, and store at room temperature for 1 day. Serve the remaining 4 slices with vanilla ice cream or sweetened whipped cream, if desired.

Sautéed Polenta Squares with Italian Sausage Sauce

Serves 4

A crisp square of sautéed or grilled polenta is heavenly. We made a chunky tomato sauce with Italian sausage and lots of chopped fresh parsley to spoon over the squares of polenta. Buy sweet mild or spicy hot Italian sausage, depending on your "heat" tolerance.

5 tablespoons olive oil

1 pound bulk Italian sausage

1 medium yellow onion (about 8 ounces), chopped

1 large rib celery, leaves removed, chopped

1 large carrot (5 ounces), peeled and chopped

1 can (28 ounces) diced tomatoes, with juice

1 cup coarsely chopped fresh parsley

1 pan chilled Polenta (page 54), cut into 8 squares

Salt and freshly ground pepper to taste

In a 4-quart sauté pan over medium heat, heat 1 tablespoon of the olive oil. Swirl to coat the pan. Add the sausage and sauté until the meat is no longer pink; use a metal spatula to cut the sausage into small chunks. Using a slotted spoon, transfer to a plate.

Drain off the fat and return the pan to medium heat. Add 2 tablespoons of the olive oil and sauté the onion, celery, and carrots until tender, about 5 minutes. Add the tomatoes and juice. Stir to combine and simmer, uncovered, until the sauce is thickened, about 15 minutes.

Meanwhile, preheat the oven to 275°F. In a 12-inch skillet over medium-high heat, heat the remaining 2 tablespoons oil and fry the polenta squares until lightly browned on both sides. You may need to do this in 2 batches. Place on a baking sheet and keep warm until the sauce is done.

Add the sausage and parsley to the sauce. Add salt and pepper. Stir to combine and cook until heated through, about 5 minutes. Taste the sauce and adjust the seasoning. Place 2 squares of polenta, slightly overlapping, on each plate. Spoon a generous amount of sauce over and serve immediately.

Pasta with Fennel, Endive, and Walnuts

Serves 4

This is a deliciously simple way to recycle the braised fennel from the weekend menu. In a very few minutes it becomes a wonderful vegetarian pasta entrée. This recipe uses curly endive, with its slightly bitter edge. You could substitute radicchio or Swiss chard. Use a chef's knife to shred the endive.

1½ cups (6 ounces) walnuts, coarsely
    chopped
1 tablespoon plus ½ teaspoon salt
½ cup olive oil
2 garlic cloves
1 red bell pepper, seeded, deribbed, and
    thinly sliced
1 pound curly endive, shredded
2 cups Braised Fennel and Onion with
    Tarragon (page 55)
    Freshly ground pepper to taste
1 pound rigatoni or other tubular pasta

Preheat the oven to 325°F. Spread the walnuts on a baking sheet and bake until lightly toasted, about 10 minutes. Set aside.

In an 8-quart or larger stockpot, bring 6 quarts of water to a boil over high heat. Add 1 tablespoon salt. Meanwhile, in a 10- to 12-inch skillet over medium heat, heat the olive oil. Add the garlic cloves and brown. Remove and discard. Add the bell pepper to the hot oil and sauté until slightly softened. Add the curly endive and cook, stirring frequently, until the endive has wilted. Add the fennel and onion, the ½ teaspoon salt, and the pepper, and cook until heated through. Turn off heat and cover to keep warm while cooking the pasta.

Cook the pasta until al dente (cooked through but still slightly chewy), about 10 minutes. Drain and return to the pot. Add the braised vegetables and toss. Divide among warmed pasta bowls or plates. Sprinkle each portion with toasted walnuts and serve immediately.

Roast Duck Soft Tacos

Serves 4

You've never seen these on the menu at your local fast-food Mexican restaurant, and you probably never will. One of the joys of cooking is that leftovers can be used to create better meals than most people get when they eat out. These tacos are remarkably simple to make. Just put the various ingredients in their own serving containers on the table and let everyone help themselves.

2 red bell peppers, roasted and peeled (see Cook's Notes)

3 cups thinly sliced hearts of romaine (1 large head; see Cook's Notes)

4 green onions, including green tops, thinly sliced

16 corn tortillas

Diced meat from ½ Roast Duck with Balsamic Glaze (page 53)

1 lime, cut into 8 wedges

1 cup (½ pint) sour cream

1 cup prepared salsa

Cut the peppers into thin slices. In a large serving bowl, combine them with the romaine and green onions. Toss well.

Preheat an oven to 200°F. Place the tortillas in a covered heatproof container such as a tortilla warmer or a shallow casserole with lid. Place the tortillas in the oven and heat for 20 minutes.

Place the duck meat, lime wedges, sour cream, and salsa in separate serving bowls. Let the diners spread a little sour cream on a tortilla, add a little salsa, a little duck, a little lettuce mixture, and squeeze a little lime juice over all. Roll and eat.

COOK'S NOTES: *To roast and peel bell peppers: Cut off the top and bottom of the peppers and cut the peppers into fourths. Remove the seeds and ribs. Place the peppers skin-side down over a high gas flame (or under a preheated broiler, skin-side up) until the skin is black. Place in a plastic or paper bag, close it, and let sit for 10 minutes. Scrape the blackened skin off with a paring knife (don't rinse, or much of the flavor will be lost).*

Hearts of romaine are the crisp leaves in the middle of a head of romaine lettuce.

weekend

**MEATLESS BLACK BEAN CHILI
WITH HOMINY**
CORN BREAD
LETTUCE, TOMATO, AND AVOCADO SALAD
CRUNCHY CHOCOLATE CHIP–PECAN COOKIES

monday

CHILI BURRITOS
Rewarm the chili and some soft flour
tortillas. Grate some cheese, open a
bottle of salsa, and voilà! Dinner.

wednesday

**TURKEY SANDWICHES WITH JALAPEÑO
MAYONNAISE ON CORN BREAD**
Warmed leftover corn bread, slathered
with a spicy mayonnaise, is topped with
thinly sliced smoked turkey breast and
jack cheese for a quick and delicious
meal.

thursday

SHRIMP AND CORN BREAD SALAD
Corn bread croutons are a crunchy basis
for a quick salad of shrimp and avocado
with a bright lime dressing.

Weekend menus don't always have to be formal. They can be casual and fun for family and friends, like this one. Dinner is a big pot of a meatless black bean chili. Served with freshly made corn bread and a simple green salad with avocado, this menu is a real crowd-pleaser. The finale of crunchy chocolate chip–pecan cookies will leave everyone smiling.

The chili can be cooked one day in advance, if time allows. In fact, it is even better reheated. The cookies can be baked early in the day; just keep them hidden so there are some left for dessert. The corn bread is simple and can be baked while the chili is warming. The salad dressing can be made several hours in advance and tossed with the greens and avocado just before serving.

We make a generous amount of corn bread, as it is used twice in the following week—in sandwich and salad form. The leftover chili is the basis for some dandy quick burritos.

Meatless Black Bean Chili with Hominy

Serves 4, with 3 cups reserved for Chili Burritos (page 69)

Continuing the variations on chili begun with our book The Basic Gourmet, *here is a version using dried black beans, now available in nearly every supermarket in America. Canned white or yellow hominy (specially processed corn) adds wonderful dried-corn flavor and color. As with most spicy soups and stews, this one is even better when made ahead and rewarmed.*

1 pound dried black beans
2 tablespoons vegetable oil
6 large garlic cloves, minced
2 jumbo yellow onions (about 2 pounds total), coarsely chopped
¼ cup chili con carne seasoning or chili powder
1 teaspoon red pepper flakes
1½ tablespoons sugar
¾ teaspoon dried thyme
1 teaspoon ground cumin
1 teaspoon dried oregano
1 teaspoon ground coriander
1 can (28 ounces) crushed or diced tomatoes in juice or purée
2 cans (14½ ounces *each*) vegetable broth
1 broth can of water
1 can (14½ ounces) white or yellow hominy, drained
1 teaspoon ground pepper
1 teaspoon salt or to taste (optional)
Cornmeal for thickening (optional)

Pick over the beans for any stones or other debris. Rinse the beans and set them aside.

In a 4-quart or larger nonreactive heavy saucepan over medium heat, heat the oil and sauté the garlic and onion until they are softened but not browned, 5 to 10 minutes. Add the chili con carne seasoning or chili powder, pepper flakes, sugar, thyme, cumin, oregano, and coriander. Stir and cook for 5 minutes. Add the beans, tomatoes (including the juice or purée), vegetable broth, water, and salt. Bring to a boil, reduce heat to a simmer, cover, and cook for 1½ hours, or until the beans are tender. Add the hominy and pepper. Taste for salt and add if necessary. Thicken, if desired, by adding 1 tablespoon cornmeal at a time and simmering for 5 minutes after each addition.

Set aside 3 cups of chili to cool and serve the rest. Cover, and refrigerate the reserved chili for up to 7 days.

Corn Bread

Makes two 9-by-13-inch pans, with 1½ pans reserved for Turkey Sandwiches with Jalapeño Mayonnaise on Corn Bread (page 70) and croutons for Shrimp and Corn Bread Salad (page 71)

A bowl of chili practically begs for hot corn bread as an accompaniment, even when there is hominy in the chili. Leftover corn bread can be used for imaginative sandwiches and croutons.

3 cups yellow or white cornmeal

3 cups all-purpose flour

1 tablespoon salt

1 tablespoon baking soda

2 cups (1 pint) sour cream

6 large eggs

6 tablespoons melted bacon fat or butter

2 tablespoons granulated sugar

Preheat the oven to 425°F. Spray two 9-by-13-inch baking pans with vegetable-oil cooking spray.

In a large bowl, whisk the cornmeal, flour, salt, and baking soda together. In a small bowl, whisk the sour cream and eggs together until blended, then add to the dry ingredients, stirring just to blend. Stir in the melted bacon fat or butter. Pour into the 2 prepared pans, smoothing the tops with a rubber spatula. Sprinkle with the sugar.

Bake for 16 to 18 minutes, or until a cake tester or toothpick inserted in the center of the corn bread comes out clean. Let cool slightly in the pans. Cut half of 1 pan into 1½-inch squares and serve.

When the reserved cornbread has completely cooled, cut the remainder of the first pan and one third of the second pan into ¾-inch croutons. Store in a plastic bag at room temperature for up to 7 days. Cut the remaining corn bread into 4 squares, wrap well, and freeze.

Lettuce, Tomato, and Avocado Salad

Serves 4

The heartiness of this menu is balanced by a mix of delicate leafy greens, coated with a dressing that includes sherry or balsamic vinegar and a little Dijon-style mustard. Ripe tomatoes provide color and a sweet acidity, and avocado lends its subtle flavor and incomparable texture. The flavors are intense enough to stand up to the chili and corn bread.

DRESSING:

½ cup vegetable oil

2 tablespoons sherry or balsamic vinegar

¼ teaspoon Dijon-style mustard

¼ teaspoon salt

¼ teaspoon ground pepper

10 cups torn mixed greens, such as romaine and red leaf lettuces

3 green onions, including green tops, thinly sliced

1 medium tomato (5 to 6 ounces), cut into 8 wedges

1 avocado, halved, pitted, and scooped out with a large spoon, cut into 8 wedges
Salt and freshly ground pepper

TO MAKE THE DRESSING: In a small bowl, whisk together all the dressing ingredients, or put them in a small jar with a tight-fitting lid and shake vigorously.

In a large bowl, toss the greens and green onions with three fourths of the dressing. Arrange on salad plates. Top with the tomato and avocado wedges, and drizzle the remaining dressing over them. Sprinkle a pinch of salt over each salad, and grind a little pepper over each. Serve.

Crunchy Chocolate Chip–Pecan Cookies

Makes about 30 cookies

These buttery cookies are packed with toasted pecans and chocolate chips. If you want any left for weeknight desserts, you may need to double the recipe, or hide some like we did!

1 cup (4 ounces) coarsely chopped pecans

1½ cups all-purpose flour

½ teaspoon salt

¾ teaspoon baking soda

¾ cup (1¼ sticks) unsalted butter at room temperature

¼ cup granulated sugar

½ cup packed light brown sugar

2 tablespoons milk

2 teaspoons pure vanilla extract

1½ cups (9 ounces) semisweet chocolate chips

Preheat the oven to 375°F. Spread the pecans on a baking sheet and toast for 5 minutes. Set aside to cool. Butter 2 baking sheets or line them with parchment paper.

Sift the flour, salt, and baking soda together into a medium bowl. In a large bowl, cream the butter and sugars together until light and fluffy, using a wooden spoon or electric mixer. Stir in the milk and vanilla until blended. Stir in the flour mixture just until blended. Stir in the pecans and chocolate chips.

Drop rounded tablespoonfuls of dough several inches apart on the prepared pans. Bake until toasty brown, about 10 to 12 minutes. Transfer to wire racks to cool completely. Store in an airtight container.

COOK'S NOTE   *These cookies freeze beautifully. If you like, double the recipe and keep a batch of the baked cookies in the freezer.*

Chili Burritos

Serves 4

Faster to make than driving through a fast-food take-out line, these burritos are unbelievably delicious, and cleanup is a snap.

4 large flour tortillas, 9 to 10 inches in diameter
3 cups Meatless Black Bean Chili with Hominy (page 65)
3 green onions, white part chopped and green part thinly sliced (reserve separately)
1½ cups (3 ounces) shredded sharp Cheddar cheese
⅓ cup chopped fresh cilantro (optional)
½ cup sour cream
1 jar mild or hot salsa

Preheat the oven to 300°F. Wrap the tortillas in aluminum foil and heat in the oven for 10 minutes. Reheat the chili.

Place a tortilla on each of 4 warmed plates. Portion one fourth of the chili onto one side of each tortilla. Scatter the chopped white part of the green onions, the cheese, and cilantro over the chili, and fold each tortilla over to cover the chili mixture. Top with a little sour cream and garnish with the sliced green onion tops. Serve with salsa on the side.

Turkey Sandwiches with Jalapeño Mayonnaise on Corn Bread

Serves 4

Being in possession of some leftover corn bread means, among other things, that you have a fine sandwich in the making. You'll have the delightful crunch and seductive flavor of ground corn plus, in this case, smoked turkey and jack cheese. It's good without the spicy mayo, but even better with it. Serve with assorted pickles and olives. Or, make a quick slaw by combining shredded cabbage with just a hint of vinegar and a little extra-virgin olive oil, plus some salt and pepper.

4 4-inch squares Corn Bread (page 66)
½ cup mayonnaise
2 tablespoons finely chopped yellow onion
1 jalapeño chili, seeded and minced
½ cup lightly packed fresh cilantro leaves, minced
12 ounces thinly sliced smoked turkey breast
4 ounces Monterey jack cheese, thinly sliced

Cut the corn bread pieces in half horizontally. In a small bowl, mix the mayonnaise, onion, jalapeño, and cilantro. Spread on the cut surfaces of the corn bread. Fold the turkey slices, if necessary, so they just overhang the corn bread. Top the turkey with the cheese slices. Place the tops on sandwiches, slice in half diagonally, and arrange on plates opened up in a V shape to provide room for pickles and olives or slaw.

Shrimp and Corn Bread Salad

Serves 4

Corn bread croutons, shrimp, cilantro, avocado, chilies, and green onions make a spicy salad, dressed with a tangy lime dressing.

8 cups ¾-inch dice Corn Bread (page 66)

8 ounces bay (tiny cooked) shrimp meat

1 cup lightly packed fresh cilantro leaves, chopped, plus cilantro sprigs for garnish

2 serrano chilies, seeded, and minced

4 green onions, including green tops, sliced

2 firm-ripe avocados, halved, pitted, scooped from peel, and cut into medium dice

½ cup extra-virgin olive oil

2 tablespoons fresh lime juice

Salt and freshly ground pepper to taste

Leaves from 1 head butter or leaf lettuce

4 lime wedges

Preheat the oven to 250°F. Spread the diced corn bread in a large baking pan and dry in the oven for 1¼ hours, stirring once or twice.

In a large bowl, toss the shrimp, chopped cilantro, chilies, green onions, and avocados together. In a small bowl or screw-top jar, whisk or shake oil, lime juice, salt, and pepper together. Pour over the shrimp mixture and toss thoroughly. Add the corn bread cubes, toss well, and divide over the lettuce leaves on plates. Put a lime wedge on each plate, along with a sprig of cilantro. Serve at once.

weekend

**BROILED FLANK STEAK WITH
SOY-HONEY MARINADE**
CURRIED ROASTED POTATOES
OVEN-BAKED TOMATOES
MIXED FRUIT COMPOTE

monday

**FLANK STEAK, POTATO, AND
ROASTED RED PEPPER SALAD**
This is a decidedly Western beef salad.
The beef and potatoes are combined with
red bell pepper, fresh tomatoes, capers,
and green onions, then tossed with a light
lime-based dressing to which a little curry
has been added.

wednesday

TOMATO-BREAD SOUP WITH PARMESAN
This hearty vegetarian soup takes its
inspiration from Italian peasant cuisine.
The roasted tomatoes are combined with
stale country-style bread, garlic, olive oil,
and a dab of pesto to make a soup so
thick your spoon will stand up in it.

thursday

**BUCKWHEAT SOBA WITH SLIVERED
FLANK STEAK, GREEN ONIONS, AND
ORANGE ZEST**
Make a marvelous Asian-style salad with
buckwheat soba noodles and a light Asian
dressing, leftover flank steak, and a bit of
carrot and green onions.

If cooked quickly, flank steak is absolutely delicious. In this preparation, the steak is first marinated in a soy-honey glaze, then broiled. This entrée is simple enough that it could be done on a weeknight as well. The steak is served with roasted curried new potatoes and with roasted tomatoes redolent of garlic and olive oil. The meal finishes with a creamy fruit compote that can be made in any season, as it relies mainly on dried fruits.

The fruit compote can be made early on the day of serving. If you want to serve it warm, add the fresh fruit just before serving. Begin marinating the flank steak 1 to 2 hours before broiling. Roast the potatoes and tomatoes at the same time, just before cooking the steak. Finish the tomatoes under the broiler, then leave the broiler on to cook the steak. Keep the vegetables warm in the meantime.

Flank steak provides great leftovers, especially for salads. We have two salads in this week of menus, one Asian and one very American. The leftover tomatoes make a great vegetarian soup.

Broiled Flank Steak with Soy-Honey Marinade

Serves 4, with 1 flank steak reserved for Flank Steak, Potato, and Roasted Red Pepper Salad (page 79) and for Buckwheat Soba with Slivered Flank Steak, Green Onions, and Orange Zest (page 81)

Planning ahead for some good leftovers, we chose an Asian-style marinade for the flank steaks. This weekend dish is a snap for any cook.

2 flank steaks (about 3½ pounds total), trimmed of fat	Put the flank steaks in a large, heavy-duty lock-top plastic bag.

MARINADE:

½ cup low-salt soy sauce

½ cup rice vinegar

⅓ cup honey

2 teaspoons ground pepper

3 tablespoons minced fresh ginger

TO MAKE THE MARINADE: Combine the marinade ingredients in a 2-cup glass measure. Pour out and reserve ⅓ cup of the marinade. Pour the marinade over the flank steaks and seal the bag, pressing out any air (this allows the marinade to fully coat the meat). Set aside at room temperature for 1 hour, or refrigerate for up to 2 hours. Turn the bag over every 15 minutes or so, to fully distribute the marinade.

About 20 minutes before serving, preheat the broiler. Remove the flank steaks from the marinade and place them side by side on a broiler pan. Broil the steaks 2 to 3 inches from the heating element for 6 minutes on the first side, then turn, brush with the reserved marinade, and broil 6 minutes longer, or until an instant-read thermometer registers 125°F. (This timing is for medium rare; add a minute to each side if you want the meat more well done.)

Set aside one of the flank steaks to cool. Transfer the other flank steak to a carving board. Let rest for 3 minutes, then slice across the grain into ¼-inch-thick slices. Serve immediately. Cut the reserved steak in half, wrap separately, and refrigerate for up to 5 days.

COOK'S NOTE   *If you love to grill, by all means fire up your grill and cook the flank steaks over hot coals. Grill on one side for 5 minutes, then turn and cook for about 4 minutes on the second side, or until an instant-read thermometer registers 125°F.*

Curried Roasted Potatoes

Serves 4, with 16 potatoes reserved for Flank Steak, Potato, and Roasted Red Pepper Salad (page 79)

Small potatoes add an appealing look and flavor to the flank steak dinner, and provide the basis for flank steak salad another day.

4 tablespoons (½ stick) unsalted butter

1 tablespoon curry powder

32 small red or white new potatoes, about 1½ inches in diameter (about 3⅓ pounds), scrubbed

Salt to taste

Preheat the oven to 350°F. In a large ovenproof skillet or sauté pan, melt the butter over medium-high heat. Stir the curry powder into the butter and cook for about 30 seconds. Add the potatoes and a sprinkling of salt. Cook for about 3 minutes, swirling the pan to turn the potatoes and coat them with curry butter, or turn them with tongs if necessary. Transfer the pan to the oven and roast, uncovered, until a cake tester or toothpick inserted in a potato slides in without resistance, about 30 minutes.

Set aside 16 potatoes to cool and serve the rest. Wrap the reserved potatoes and refrigerate for up to 7 days.

Oven-Baked Tomatoes

Serves 4, with 8 tomato halves and pan juices reserved for Tomato-Bread Soup with Parmesan (page 80)

Hothouse tomatoes are increasingly popular, and their flavor is worth paying for. We suggest buying them during the majority of the year, when ordinary tomatoes are never really ripe.

8 tomatoes, about 5 or 6 ounces each
3 garlic cloves, minced
3 tablespoons extra-virgin olive oil
  Salt and freshly ground pepper to taste

Preheat the oven to 350°F. Cut a tiny slice off the bottom of each tomato so it can sit upright. Cut the tomatoes in half horizontally. Arrange in a 9-by-13-inch baking dish. Mix the garlic and olive oil and drizzle over each tomato. Sprinkle with salt and pepper. Bake for 30 minutes.

Remove the pan from the oven, preheat the broiler, and position a rack as close to the heat source as possible. Place the tomatoes under the broiler until lightly browned, about 2 minutes. Serve 2 tomato halves per person.

Set aside 8 tomato halves and the pan juices to cool. Cover and refrigerate the reserved tomatoes and juice for up to 7 days.

Mixed Fruit Compote

Serves 4

This puddinglike compote includes both dried and fresh fruits, as well as cream, and can be made several days in advance. The fresh fruit is added just before serving, and it is topped with whipped cream.

6 ounces pitted prunes
4 ounces dried peaches
3 ounces dried cranberries
3 cups water
½ cinnamon stick
6 tablespoons granulated sugar
2 tablespoons all-purpose flour
6 tablespoons plus ½ cup heavy (whipping) cream
2 tablespoons bourbon whiskey
1 firm, ripe pear, cored and cut into 1-inch pieces
1 ripe peach, peeled, cored, and cut into 1-inch pieces

In a 2-quart saucepan, combine the prunes, dried peaches, dried cranberries, water, and cinnamon stick. Bring to a boil over medium-high heat, reduce to a simmer, cover, and cook for 10 minutes.

While the fruit is cooking, whisk the sugar and flour together in a medium bowl. Add the 6 tablespoons cream and whisk until smooth.

When the fruit has cooked, stir the cream mixture into the pan. Bring to a simmer and cook for about 2 minutes. Add the bourbon. Remove from heat.

Serve warm, at room temperature, or chilled. Stir the fresh fruit into the compote just before serving and ladle into serving bowls. In a deep bowl, beat the ½ cup cream until soft peaks form. Serve over the compote.

Flank Steak, Potato, and Roasted Red Pepper Salad

Serves 4

This entrée salad of cold cooked steak, roasted potatoes, and roasted peppers is quite a satisfying meal.

½ Broiled Flank Steak with Soy-Honey
   Marinade (page 75)
2 large red bell peppers, roasted and
   peeled (see page 61)
16 Curried Roasted Potatoes (page 76),
   quartered
3 green onions, including green tops,
   thinly sliced
2 small tomatoes, cut into 10 wedges each
2 tablespoons capers, drained
1 cup lightly packed fresh parsley leaves,
   minced
¼ teaspoon salt
   Freshly ground pepper to taste
   Leaves from 1 head red leaf lettuce

With a sharp chef's knife, cut the steak in half horizontally to make 2 thinner pieces of the same shape you started with. Cut the steak with the grain to make several strips about 1 inch wide. Turn each strip and cut across the grain in very thin (about ⅛ inch) slices. This sort of French fry shape is known as "julienne." Cut the peppers into the same shape as the beef.

In a large bowl, combine the potatoes, bell peppers, green onions, tomatoes, capers, parsley, salt, and pepper. Toss to blend.

DRESSING:

2 tablespoons fresh lemon juice
6 tablespoons extra-virgin olive oil
½ teaspoon curry powder
⅛ teaspoon salt
   Freshly ground pepper to taste

TO MAKE THE DRESSING: Whisk the dressing ingredients together and pour over salad. Arrange the lettuce on 4 dinner plates, then top with the salad mixture. Top with the beef and serve.

Tomato-Bread Soup with Parmesan

Serves 4

This soup is thick, satisfying, and ready to serve in about thirty minutes.

---

  8 halves Oven-Baked Tomatoes (page 77)
     and reserved pan juices
 ¼ cup olive oil
  1 large garlic clove, slivered
5½ cups water, or more as needed
  1 pound crusty bread, roughly torn into
     1-inch pieces
  2 teaspoons salt
  1 teaspoon ground pepper
 ¼ cup Pesto (page 121) or prepared pesto
  2 cups (8 ounces) grated Parmesan cheese

Use a spoon to scoop the pulp and juices from the tomato skins into a bowl. Discard the skins. In a heavy 4-quart or larger saucepan over medium heat, heat the olive oil and sauté the garlic just until it begins to brown, 1 to 2 minutes. Add the tomatoes and juices, bring to a boil, reduce heat to a simmer, and cover. Cook for 15 minutes. Add the water, bread, salt, and pepper. Bring the soup to a simmer. Add more water if necessary to create a thick soup rather than a mush. Stir in the pesto. Taste and adjust the seasoning. Portion into 4 large soup plates or bowls and top with ½ cup grated Parmesan per portion.

Buckwheat Soba with Slivered Flank Steak, Green Onions, and Orange Zest

Serves 4

Buckwheat soba, or Japanese buckwheat noodles, pair beautifully with slivers of beef, rounds of green onion, and a hint of orange. If you can't find soba, purchase any thin wheat-based noodle. This salad is best served at room temperature.

¼ cup soy sauce

1 tablespoon rice vinegar

2 tablespoons Asian sesame oil

2 teaspoons granulated sugar

1 teaspoon freshly grated orange zest

1 tablespoon salt

1 package (14 ounces) buckwheat soba noodles

2 green onions, including green tops, cut into paper-thin diagonal slices

¾ cup shredded or matchstick-cut carrot

½ Flank Steak with Soy-Honey Marinade (page 75), cut into matchstick-size slivers

Fill an 8-quart stockpot three-quarters full of water, cover, and bring to a boil. In a large bowl, combine the soy sauce, vinegar, sesame oil, sugar, and orange zest. Stir to combine and dissolve the sugar, then set aside.

Add the salt to the boiling water and cook the noodles until cooked through but still slightly chewy, 6 to 7 minutes. They shouldn't be mushy, but if they have a crunchy, raw center, cook for 1 to 2 minutes longer, and taste again.

Drain off about 1 quart of the pasta water, then add about 1 quart of ice cold water to the pot, stir the noodles, then immediately drain the noodles thoroughly in a colander. Add the noodles to the soy dressing and toss well. Add the green onions, carrots, and flank steak. Toss to combine. Taste and adjust the seasoning. Serve immediately.

Salmon is the king of fishes. Chinook (King) and Coho (silver) salmon are the most sought-after varieties, but any salmon roasts nicely and provides fabulous leftovers. We accompany our beautiful salmon with a simple lemon-garlic couscous and some crunchy snow peas. Dessert is seductively crunchy Chocolate–Chocolate Chip Biscotti.

The biscotti can be made the morning of serving, or as much as one week in advance. The couscous and snow peas cook quickly while the salmon is roasting. Make sure to allow time for the salmon to rest to allow its juices to set.

weekend

WHOLE ROAST SALMON
LEMON-GARLIC COUSCOUS
CRUNCHY SNOW PEAS
CHOCOLATE–CHOCOLATE CHIP BISCOTTI

monday

SALMON HASH
The remainder of our fancy salmon goes "down home" in a one-dish meal that includes diced potatoes, onion, celery, and herbs.

wednesday

COUSCOUS SALAD WITH CASHEWS, CURRANTS, AND SNOW PEAS
Leftover couscous and snow peas are the basis for a quick and appealing weeknight salad supper, with the addition of some crunchy cashews, currants, and a lemon and olive oil dressing.

thursday

RISOTTO WITH SALMON, PARSLEY, AND GREEN ONIONS
About 30 minutes of cutting and stirring produces a creamy dish to which you add flaked salmon at the last minute.

Whole Roast Salmon

Serves 4, with half reserved for Risotto with Salmon, Parsley, and Green Onions (page 91) and for Salmon Hash (page 88)

A magnificent presentation for salmon-lovers, a whole roast fish is not at all difficult to do.

1 whole salmon (5 to 7 pounds), cleaned,
   head and tail on
   Salt and freshly ground pepper to taste
1 lemon, cut into 8 wedges
1 large onion (10 to 12 ounces), cut into
   1-inch wedges
1 cup dry white wine
½ cup heavy (whipping) cream

Preheat the oven to 400°F. Line a large roasting pan with foil and spray the foil with vegetable-oil cooking spray (or use a nonstick baking pan). Place the fish on the pan, diagonally if necessary. If the fish is still too large, cut off the head and tail using a sharp chef's knife. Using a ruler, measure the fish at its thickest part. Turn the fish on its back, spread the cavity open and sprinkle with salt and pepper. Toss the lemon and onion wedges together and stuff them inside the fish. Lay the fish on its side. Pour the wine over the fish and cover with foil that has been sprayed with vegetable-oil cooking spray.

Place the pan in the oven and bake the fish for 10 minutes for every inch of thickness before testing for doneness. For example, if the fish is 4 inches thick at its thickest point (just behind the head), then bake it 40 minutes before testing. Insert an instant-read thermometer in the thickest part; when it registers 130° to 140°F, the fish is done. Remove the pan from the oven. Tilt the pan while restraining the fish and pour the pan juices into a 1-quart saucepan, or use a bulb baster or serving spoon to collect the juices. Cover the salmon loosely with foil and let sit for 10 minutes before carving, to allow the juices to set.

While the salmon rests, add the cream to the salmon juices in the saucepan and bring to a boil over medium-high heat. Cook at a slow boil (take care it doesn't boil over) until thickened enough to coat a spoon. Pour the sauce into a small warm sauceboat or pitcher for passing at the table.

Peel the skin off the fish and slide it carefully onto a carving board. Use a carving knife to cut gently along the seam running lengthwise down the middle of the side of fish, then cut each of those 2 pieces crosswise into serving portions, using a knife and serving spatula to lift the pieces of fish away from the bone, and serve, leaving the bottom half of the fish to cool.

After the meal, cut through the backbone of the salmon just behind head, then gently lift out the entire bone structure and discard. Lift, bone, and flake the flesh into ½-inch flakes. Wrap and refrigerate for up to 4 days.

Lemon-Garlic Couscous

Serves 4, with 6 cups reserved for Couscous Salad with Cashews, Currants, and Snow Peas (page 89)

Our book The Basic Gourmet Entertains *has a simple recipe for couscous made with apricots and pine nuts. This version is even easier. Couscous—actually a tiny pasta—is filling and lends itself to many styles of cooking.*

2   tablespoons olive oil
4   garlic cloves, minced
    Minced zest and juice of 1 lemon
7   cups Chicken Stock (page 23) or
    canned low-salt chicken broth
3   boxes (10 ounces each) quick-cooking
    couscous (see Cook's Note)
    Salt and freshly ground pepper to taste
1   cup lightly packed fresh parsley leaves,
    coarsely chopped

In a 6-quart or larger heavy saucepan over medium heat, heat the olive oil and sauté the garlic just until it starts to color. Add the lemon zest, lemon juice, and stock. Bring to a boil over medium-high heat. Stir in the couscous, cover, and turn off heat. Let sit for 5 minutes. Use a fork to fluff the couscous. Add salt, pepper, and parsley. Set aside 6 cups couscous to cool and serve the rest. Cover and refrigerate the reserved couscous for up to 7 days.

COOK'S NOTE   *Couscous is often sold in 10-ounce boxes that are labeled as flavored in various ways. If you cannot find plain, unseasoned couscous, just buy any box and discard the seasoning packet inside.*

Crunchy Snow Peas

Serves 4, with 2 cups reserved for Couscous Salad with Cashews, Currants, and Snow Peas (page 89)

Available year-round, snow peas are an easy and pretty side dish.

1¼ pounds fresh snow peas, stem end
    trimmed and strings removed
1 teaspoon salt

Rinse the snow peas in a colander and set aside. Fill a 6- to 8-quart saucepan three-fourths full with water and bring to a boil. Three minutes before serving the entrée, add the salt to the boiling water, then add the snow peas. Boil for 2 minutes, then drain in a colander.

Plunge 2 cups of the snow peas into cold water and serve the rest. Drain the reserved snow peas on paper towels, and refrigerate for up to 5 days.

COOK'S NOTE   *In the spring, look for sugar snap peas and use them instead. Cook sugar snap peas for 3 to 4 minutes, or until crisp-tender.*

Chocolate–Chocolate Chip Biscotti

Makes 26 to 30 biscotti

After salmon and couscous, close the meal with a crunchy dark chocolate cookie. Serve a cup of coffee, and dessert is complete.

4 tablespoons (½ stick) unsalted butter at
   room temperature
¾ cup granulated sugar
2 large eggs
1 teaspoon pure vanilla extract
1¾ cups all-purpose flour
¼ cup unsweetened cocoa powder
1½ teaspoons baking powder
½ teaspoon salt
1 cup semisweet chocolate chips

Preheat the oven to 350°F. In a large bowl, cream the butter and sugar together until light and fluffy using a wooden spoon or an electric mixer. Beat in the eggs one at a time. Mix in the vanilla. Sift the flour, cocoa, baking powder, and salt together onto a sheet of waxed paper. Add to the wet ingredients and stir until blended. Stir the chocolate chips into the dough.

Turn the mixture out onto a floured work surface. The dough will be quite sticky. Divide the dough in half. With floured hands, roll each half into a flattened log 1½ inches thick and 10 to 11 inches long. Place both logs about 3 inches apart on a nonstick or parchment-lined baking sheet. Bake until lightly firm to the touch, about 25 minutes. Remove from the oven and let sit for 5 minutes.

Place a log on a cutting board. With a serrated knife, and using a sawing motion, carefully cut the log on the diagonal into ¾-inch-thick slices. Place the slices on the baking sheet. Repeat with the second log. Bake for 5 minutes. Turn each slice over and bake 10 minutes longer. Transfer to wire racks to cool completely. Store up to 1 week in a tightly covered container at room temperature.

COOK'S NOTE   *If you love nuts, add ¼ cup toasted chopped walnuts or pecans. To toast, place the nuts on a baking sheet and toast in a preheated 350°F oven until lightly brown and fragrant, about 5 minutes. Let cool, then add to the dough along with the chocolate chips.*

Salmon Hash

Serves 4

Leftover cooked meats and fish of all kinds can be transformed into one of the world's most humble but satisfying dishes: hash. Generally speaking, hash includes potatoes as a primary ingredient, along with onion and sometimes other vegetables. This version uses our tried-and-true potato-onion-celery combination. Be sure to check the fish for bones before adding it to the pan.

4 tablespoons (½ stick) unsalted butter

2 pounds firm-fleshed potatoes (such as White Rose, Yukon Gold, Yellow Finn), peeled and cut into ½-inch dice

1 large yellow onion (10 to 12 ounces), cut into ½-inch dice

2 ribs celery, halved lengthwise, and cut crosswise into ⅛-inch slices

¼ teaspoon dried dill weed

½ teaspoon dried thyme

¼ teaspoon salt

½ teaspoon ground pepper

3½ cups flaked Whole Roast Salmon (page 84)

1 cup lightly packed fresh parsley leaves, coarsely chopped

Ketchup for serving

In a 12-inch and preferably nonstick skillet or sauté pan, melt the butter over medium heat. Add all the ingredients except the salmon and the parsley. Cover and cook for 10 minutes to steam the potatoes. Uncover, raise the heat to medium-high, and stir the mixture. Cook, stirring every 5 minutes, until lightly browned, about 25 minutes. Taste for salt, adding more if desired. Add the salmon and parsley and cook until the salmon is just warmed through. Serve from the pan at the table, or serve on 4 warmed plates. Ketchup is the traditional accompaniment.

Couscous Salad with Cashews, Currants, and Snow Peas

Serves 4 as an entrée, or about 12 as part of a buffet

Like other pastas, couscous is easy to turn into a salad. The addition of cashews, currants, and snow peas adds an appealing nutty crunch, dried-fruit sweetness, and fresh-vegetable crispness. The salad is a great family entrée, and also makes a fine addition to a buffet table for brunch, lunch, or dinner entertaining.

1 cup dried currants or raisins, soaked in hot water for 30 minutes and drained

6 cups Lemon-Garlic Couscous (page 85)

2 cups Crunchy Snow Peas (page 86)

2 cups (10 to 12 ounces) salted roasted cashews

4 green onions, including green tops, thinly sliced

½ teaspoon salt

Freshly ground black pepper to taste

Leaves of 1 head butter or leaf lettuce for serving

In a large bowl, combine the currants, couscous, peas, cashews, green onions, salt, and pepper. Toss to mix.

DRESSING:

½ cup plus 2 tablespoons extra-virgin olive oil

2 tablespoons fresh lemon juice

2 garlic cloves, minced

¼ teaspoon cayenne pepper

¼ teaspoon salt

½ teaspoon ground pepper

TO MAKE THE DRESSING: Whisk together all the dressing ingredients, pour onto the salad, and toss the salad again. Taste for salt and pepper, adding more if necessary. Serve on lettuce leaves on individual plates, or on a platter.

Risotto with Salmon, Parsley, and Green Onions

Serves 4

After a long day of work, sipping a glass of white wine while stirring risotto is a treat. Ten minutes with a knife and cutting board and 20 minutes at the stove is all you need for this comforting dish.

5 cups Chicken Stock (page 23) or low-
  salt canned chicken broth
3 tablespoons olive oil
⅓ cup finely chopped white onion
1½ cups Arborio rice (see Cook's Note)
½ cup dry white wine
1½ cups flaked Whole Roast Salmon
  (page 84)
⅓ cup minced fresh parsley
½ cup heavy (whipping) cream
2 tablespoons finely chopped green onion
  tops

Bring the stock or broth to a simmer. In a 3-quart heavy saucepan over medium heat, heat the oil and sauté the onion until translucent, about 3 minutes. Add the rice and stir until the grains are well coated with oil, about 1 minute. Add the wine and let come to a boil.

Add ½ cup stock or broth to the rice and cook, stirring frequently, until the rice has almost completely absorbed the liquid. Adjust the heat so the risotto is kept at a slow simmer. Repeat, adding ½ cup stock or broth at a time and reserving ¼ cup. After about 18 minutes, the rice will be plump and cooked through but still slightly chewy.

Add the salmon, parsley, cream, minced green onion, and the remaining ¼ cup stock or broth. Stir gently for 1 to 2 minutes, allowing some of the cream to be absorbed and the salmon to heat through. Spoon the risotto into warm flat bowls and serve immediately.

COOK'S NOTE   *Look in the specialty grain section of your supermarket for Arborio rice. Otherwise, it is readily available at specialty stores carrying Italian foodstuffs.*

weekend

STANDING RIB ROAST (PRIME RIB)
CLASSIC MASHED POTATOES
CARAMELIZED ONIONS AND CARROTS
COFFEE GRANITA WITH CHOCOLATE SAUCE

monday

POTATO PANCAKES
APPLE AND BLUE CHEESE SALAD
WITH PECANS
Leftover mashed potatoes make comforting and homey potato pancakes.

tuesday

PASTA WITH PORCINI MUSHROOMS, CARAMELIZED ONIONS, AND CARROTS
For this week, another vegetarian entrée is made from the vegetable sauté. The addition of dried porcini adds a hearty, robust undertone.

wednesday

PAPRIKA BEEF WITH MUSHROOMS
Slices of roast beef are incorporated at the last minute into a mildly spicy sauce and served over broad egg noodles.

thursday

PRIME RIB SANDWICHES
What could be better—a simple, hearty, roast beef sandwich on great bread, spiced with horseradish.

It is hard to think of a grander entrée presentation than a standing rib roast (prime rib of beef). But don't worry; even though it is impressive, it is just a roast. Mashed potatoes are a classic accompaniment. A sauté of onions and carrots adds a sweet note to the dinner plate. The dessert is light and delicious after the filling main course. Our coffee granita is simply sugar and brewed coffee frozen in the freezer, then gilded with a luscious choco-late sauce.

Make the granita and the chocolate sauce the morning of the dinner. The sauce can even be made several days ahead. The roast will take about three and a half hours in the oven. About one hour before serving, cook and mash the potatoes and, finally, sauté the vegetables.

A seven-pound roast will provide lots of leftovers, which should be properly wrapped and promptly refrigerated after the meal. Here are ideas for four weeknight dinners using this menu: two from the beef, one from the potatoes, and one from the vegetable sauté.

Standing Rib Roast (Prime Rib)

Serves 4 (eight ½-inch slices), with the rest reserved for Paprika Beef with Mushrooms (page 102), and Prime Rib Sandwiches (page 103)

Surely the king of beef roasts, a standing rib roast is a visual tour de force that is easier to carve than roast chicken. All it requires is a few hours of roasting and a sharp carving knife. Leftovers can easily be turned into world-class roast beef sandwiches and a whole series of main dishes.

1 standing rib roast of beef (5 ribs),
   preferably small end, rack of bones
   removed and tied onto roast
½ teaspoon salt
1½ teaspoons ground pepper
   Prepared horseradish for serving
   (optional)

Buy the roast from a market selling USDA Choice (or, even better, Prime) beef, if possible. It will be juicer and more tender than lesser grades, often tagged "select" or some other meaningless term. Be sure the chine bone, feather bones, and back strap have been removed for easy carving. Tell the butcher to remove the rack of rib bones, then tie it back on with butcher's twine. Cooking the roast with the ribs tied on helps make it even more tender and juicy.

Preheat the oven to 200°F. Rub the salt and pepper over all the sides of the roast. Place the roast, bone-side down, on a rack in a roasting pan or another large pan with sides at least 1 inch high. Place the pan in the lower third of the oven. Bake for 3 to 3½ hours (25 to 30 minutes per pound) for medium rare, but test for doneness about 20 minutes *before* you expect the roast to be done. An instant-read thermometer should register 120° to 130°F when inserted into the center of the meat. Let rest for 10 minutes before carving to minimize juice loss.

Place the roast on a carving board, bone-side up. Cut the twine and remove the rib-bone rack. The bones may be separated and served with the roast, or reserved for another meal (see Cook's Notes). Turn the roast so the fat side is up and use a very sharp carving knife to cut eight ½-inch slices. Serve 2 slices per person. Pass a small bowl of prepared horseradish—many people love it with roast beef. Cool, wrap, and refrigerate the remaining beef for up to 7 days.

COOK'S NOTES   *If the bones are not served, save them in the freezer until you have 2 or more bones for each person. Roast the bones in a preheated 250°F oven until the meat is tender, about 1½ hours. Serve with barbecue sauce or spicy mustard.*

    Knowing the accuracy of your oven is important for low-temperature roasting. Roasting at less than 200°F is not safe, so check your oven using a good oven thermometer (see page 12).

Classic Mashed Potatoes

Serves 4, with 2½ cups reserved for Potato Pancakes (page 99)

Mashed potatoes are always a welcome side dish, and with a roast prime rib they are a classic accompaniment.

6 large russet potatoes (about 4½ pounds total), peeled and rinsed
1½ cups milk
¾ cup (1½ sticks) unsalted butter
Salt and freshly ground pepper to taste

Cut each potato into 4 or 5 large chunks and place in a 4-quart saucepan. Add cold water to cover, cover the pot, and bring the water to a boil. Uncover and reduce heat so the water boils gently. Cook until potatoes are tender but not mushy when pierced with a fork, 10 to 12 minutes. Meanwhile, heat the milk and butter in a small saucepan until hot but not boiling.

Drain the potatoes, return them to the pan, and toss them over low heat for a minute or so to evaporate the excess water. Remove from heat and mash the potatoes in the pan using a masher or even a strong wire whisk, or force them through a ricer into a warm bowl. Gradually whisk the milk mixture into the potatoes until they are the consistency you prefer. Add salt and pepper.

Set aside 2½ cups of the potatoes to cool and serve the rest. Cover and refrigerate the reserved potatoes for up to 5 days.

COOK'S NOTE   *Mashed potatoes may be cooked and mashed 30 to 45 minutes in advance and kept warm in a covered heatproof glass or stainless steel bowl set over barely simmering water in a saucepan. Or, they may be reheated just before serving in a microwave-safe bowl in a microwave oven.*

Caramelized Onions and Carrots

Serves 4, with 2 cups reserved for Pasta with Porcini Mushrooms, Caramelized Onions, and Carrots (page 101)

If you are making this menu in winter, here is a colorful vegetable dish to dress up the plate. In the late spring, if sweet onions such as Vidalia or Walla Walla are available, substitute them for the yellow onions.

1½ tablespoons unsalted butter

1½ tablespoons olive oil

12 medium carrots (about 1½ pounds), peeled and cut into ¼-inch-thick rounds

3 large yellow onions (about 2½ pounds), cut into thin wedges

2 tablespoons granulated sugar

1 teaspoon salt

Freshly ground pepper to taste

⅓ cup minced fresh parsley

In a large sauté pan or skillet, melt the butter with the olive oil over high heat. Swirl to coat the pan, add the carrots and onions, and sauté, stirring constantly, for 2 minutes. Reduce heat to medium, cover the pan, and cook for 10 minutes. Uncover the pan, increase heat to high, and add the sugar, salt, and pepper. Sauté until the vegetables are lightly caramelized, about 5 minutes. Add the parsley, and stir to combine.

Set aside 2 cups of the onions and carrots to cool and serve the rest. Cover and refrigerate the reserved vegetables for up to 3 days.

Coffee Granita with Chocolate Sauce

Serves 4

Granita is an Italian ice that is so simple to make and so delicious you will be amazed. It takes just a couple of hours in a home freezer. Buy the best-quality coffee you can find and brew it strong. The splendid chocolate sauce adds a sophisticated touch; then we further gild the lily with fresh raspberries and whipped cream.

This dessert is light, rich, and refreshing all at the same time. Don't hesitate to vary the fruit at different times of the year—try fresh mandarins in winter, for example. The leftover chocolate sauce will keep, covered, in the refrigerator for a couple of weeks. (A lovely dessert later in the week would be chocolate sauce over good-quality coffee ice cream with ripe banana slices.) The granita is best served the day it is made.

CHOCOLATE SAUCE

- 4 ounces unsweetened chocolate, chopped
- 2 tablespoons unsalted butter
- 1 cup heavy (whipping) cream
- ¾ cup granulated sugar
- ¼ teaspoon salt
- ½ teaspoon pure vanilla extract

- ¾ cup granulated sugar
- 4 cups strong brewed coffee, cooled
- 1 cup (½ pint) heavy (whipping) cream, well chilled
- 1 tablespoon granulated sugar
- ½ teaspoon pure vanilla extract
- 1 cup (½ pint) fresh raspberries or other seasonal fruit

TO MAKE THE CHOCOLATE SAUCE: In a small saucepan, melt the chocolate and butter over very low heat. Add the cream, sugar, and salt. Stir until the sugar is dissolved and the sauce is smooth. Leave on heat for a few minutes longer to thicken slightly. Remove from heat and add the vanilla extract. Let cool to room temperature.

Stir the sugar into the cool coffee and pour into a shallow metal baking dish. Place in the freezer and stir every 30 minutes until the ice is chunky, about 3 hours.

In a chilled deep bowl, combine the cream, sugar, and vanilla. Beat until soft peaks form.

To assemble, place about ½ cup coffee ice in each individual serving bowl or wineglass (very pretty). Sprinkle each with a few raspberries. Top with 2 tablespoons chocolate sauce and a dollop of softly whipped cream. Serve immediately, as granita melts very quickly.

Potato Pancakes

Serves 4

Nothing more than leftover mashed potatoes, a little flour, an egg, and some bread crumbs, these pancakes fry up beautifully brown and crisp on the outside, while remaining tender on the inside. If your leftover potatoes are watery, drain them. You may need to mix a tablespoon or more of the bread crumbs into the potatoes to firm them up a bit before forming the patties. Serve a crisp Apple and Blue Cheese Salad with Pecans (page 100) alongside.

2½ cups Classic Mashed Potatoes (page 96)
¼ cup all-purpose flour
1 egg, beaten
½ cup unseasoned dried bread crumbs
2 tablespoons vegetable oil

With wet hands, form the potatoes into 4 patties about 1 inch thick. They will be very soft. Place the flour, egg, and crumbs in separate small, shallow bowls. Gently dredge each patty on both sides in the flour, then in the egg, and finally in the crumbs.

In a large nonstick skillet, heat the oil. Put the patties in the pan and cook, uncovered, until they are well browned on the bottom, about 10 minutes. Use 2 thin-bladed metal or plastic spatulas to carefully turn them and cook on the second side. Lower heat to medium-low if they appear to be browning too quickly. Slow cooking will produce a thicker crust and ensure that the patties are heated through. Serve hot.

Apple and Blue Cheese Salad with Pecans

Serves 4

This salad is crisp, creamy, tangy, and crunchy, all at the same time. It is a perfect accompaniment to potato pancakes. Many different blue cheeses would work in this recipe, among them Oregon blue, Maytag blue, Roquefort, Gorgonzola, Stilton, and Danish blue. Avoid soft, Brie-like cheeses.

DRESSING:

3 tablespoons olive oil
¼ teaspoon Dijon-style mustard
1½ teaspoons fresh lemon juice
¼ teaspoon ground pepper

4 sweet-tart, crisp apples such as Gala, Braeburn, Fuji, or Granny Smith, quartered, cored, and cut into large dice
1 tablespoon fresh lemon juice
½ small red onion
4 ounces blue cheese, crumbled
¼ cup pecan pieces, toasted for 10 minutes in a preheated 350°F oven
Leaves from 1 head romaine lettuce

TO MAKE THE DRESSING: Whisk all the dressing ingredients together in a small bowl.

In a medium bowl, toss the apples in the lemon juice. Cut the onion half into very thin slices and add to the apples. Add the blue cheese, pecans, and dressing. Toss well. Arrange the romaine leaves on salad plates and top with the salad. Serve.

Pasta with Porcini Mushrooms, Caramelized Onions, and Carrots

Serves 4

This is perfect cold-weather fare, as well as a vegetarian option for a weeknight meal. The robust flavors of porcini mushrooms, carrots, and onions are combined with porcini broth and minced parsley, then tossed with pasta. Serve this with a simple salad, and pour yourself a glass of Chianti while cooking.

1 ounce dried porcini mushrooms (see Cook's Note)

1¾ cup hot water

2 teaspoons salt

1 pound rigatoni or penne pasta

2 cups Caramelized Onions and Carrots (page 97)

¼ cup minced fresh parsley

Soak the dried porcini mushrooms in the hot water for 20 minutes. Meanwhile, fill an 8- to 10-quart stockpot three-fourths full with water, cover, and bring to a boil.

Lift out the mushrooms by hand, squeezing the excess liquid from them back into the soaking liquid. Save the porcini broth. Rinse the mushrooms and clean any pieces that might have soil embedded in them. Chop any large pieces and set the mushrooms aside on a plate. Filter the porcini broth through a sieve lined with a paper towel. Measure and reserve 1¾ cups.

When the water comes to a boil, add the salt to the stockpot. Add the pasta and cook until al dente (cooked through but still slightly chewy), about 10 minutes. Meanwhile, bring the reserved porcini broth to a simmer in a 2½-quart saucepan. Stir in the mushrooms and onion mixture. Heat through.

When the pasta is done, drain immediately in a colander. Return the pasta to the stockpot and add the porcini mixture. Toss to combine, add the parsley, and toss lightly. Put the pasta in warm bowls and serve immediately.

COOK'S NOTE   *Dried porcini mushrooms are available in most well-stocked groceries. Specialty stores may sell them in bulk. They are a wonderful pantry staple, so buy several packages and keep them on the shelf.*

Paprika Beef with Mushrooms

Serves 4

Leftover standing rib roast is a gold mine in the refrigerator, no doubt about it. Here is a mildly spicy and satisfying dish using cooked medium-rare beef. Fold the beef in at the last minute. Serve this over noodles, rice, or barley.

4 tablespoons vegetable oil

1 pound white mushrooms, cut into ¼-inch-thick slices

3 ¼-inch-thick slices Standing Rib Roast (page 95)

2 medium yellow onions (about 1 pound), cut into ½-inch dice

3 tablespoons sweet Hungarian paprika

1 tablespoon hot Hungarian paprika

1 bay leaf

½ teaspoon dried thyme

1 teaspoon celery seed

2 tablespoons tomato paste

2 cans (14½ ounces *each*) beef broth

3 tablespoons all-purpose flour

1 cup (½ pint) sour cream

½ teaspoon salt

Freshly ground pepper to taste

¼ cup minced fresh parsley for garnish

Cooked egg noodles, rice, or barley for serving (see Cook's Note)

In a 12-inch heavy sauté pan or skillet, heat 2 tablespoons of the oil over medium-high heat. Add the mushrooms and sauté until they are nicely browned and their moisture has evaporated. Set aside in a medium bowl. Cut the roast beef into 1-inch-wide strips.

In the same pan, heat the remaining 2 tablespoons vegetable oil over medium heat. Add the onion and sauté until soft but not browned, about 5 minutes. Stir in the paprikas, bay leaf, thyme, and celery seed, and cook for 1 minute. Stir in the mushrooms, tomato paste, and all but ¼ cup of the beef broth. Bring to a boil, reduce heat to a simmer, cover, and cook for 10 minutes. Place the ¼ cup reserved beef broth and the flour in a small screw-top jar and shake vigorously to combine. Whisk the flour mixture into the pan and whisk for a minute or two. Simmer for 5 minutes. Stir in the sour cream, keeping the mixture at a bare simmer. Add salt and pepper. Just before serving, add the beef and heat for 1 minute. Serve.

COOK'S NOTE   *If you are serving the paprika beef over cooked dried noodles, you will need 12 ounces of noodles.*

Prime Rib Sandwiches

Serves 4

One of the simplest and best ways to eat leftover standing rib roast is to slice it thinly and place it between slices of good bread. Add a little horseradish, some sweet butter, some thinly sliced red onion, and a lettuce leaf for color and crunch, and a satisfying meal is at hand. Cranberry sauce or chutney served on the side would be perfect.

4 tablespoons (½ stick) unsalted butter at room temperature

8 ½-inch-thick slices crusty bread

4 very thin slices red onion, separated into rings

8 thin slices Standing Rib Roast (page 95)

4 large leaf lettuce leaves

Prepared horseradish

Butter 4 slices of the bread. Top with the onions, sliced beef, and lettuce leaves. Spread the horseradish on the remaining bread and top the sandwiches. Serve.

Ham is a remarkably versatile meat and can add its marvelous flavor to a wide range of crowd-pleasing dishes. The star of this weekend menu is a bourbon-glazed ham. A sweet potato sauté accompanies the ham, along with sautéed Swiss chard. Dinner ends with homemade cherry pie.

The pie should be made the morning of serving, to allow several hours to cool. Even though the ham is bought fully cooked, it must be baked for about one and a half hours to heat it through. Fifteen minutes before serving, start cooking the potatoes and greens.

If you don't want to use all five ham menus during the same week, the leftover ham can be frozen.

weekend

BOURBON-GLAZED HAM
SWEET POTATO SAUTÉ
SAUTÉED SWISS CHARD
CHERRY PIE

monday
CHEDDAR MACARONI WITH HAM
Could life be much better than a home-made cherry pie and Cheddar mac in the same week? This macaroni will feed you handsomely, with some leftover to freeze for a future "instant" meal.

tuesday

HAM, SHRIMP, AND SWEET POTATO JAMBALAYA
A mouthwatering, hearty Creole rice dish with ham and shrimp, further seasoned with leftover sautéed sweet potato.

wednesday

ASIAN NOODLE BOWL WITH HAM
A comforting Asian noodle bowl with rice noodles and earthy black mushrooms.

thursday

HAM, SWEET POTATO, AND SWISS CHARD FRITTATA
Leftover sautéed Swiss chard is paired with ham and sautéed sweet potatoes in a super-simple Italian omelet.

Bourbon-Glazed Ham

Serves 4 (8 to 12 slices total), with the rest reserved for Cheddar Macaroni with Ham (page 112), Ham, Shrimp, and Sweet Potato Jambalaya (page 113), Asian Noodle Bowl with Ham (page 114), and Ham, Sweet Potato, and Swiss Chard Frittata (page 115)

At one time, ham meant a hand-salted, smoked, bone-in rear leg of pork. It took several days of soaking, then long, slow cooking, to produce its world-famous flavor. Country ham like that is long gone, except by mail order, for most of us. If you can, find a bone-in ham without the words water added *on the label. Specialty-meat shops and even warehouse clubs can be sources for better-quality bone-in hams. If a bone-in ham is not easy to find, or if you prefer to avoid the challenge of carving, then buy a quality boneless ham. Even a "picnic ham" or "smoked pork shoulder" (the same cut) makes very good eating, and they are much smaller than a whole ham. Nearly all hams are sold and labeled as "fully cooked" today, and need only enough time in the oven to warm them through to 130°F.*

1 8- to 9-pound bone-in smoked ham
1 cup packed brown sugar
1 tablespoon dry mustard
3 tablespoons bourbon whiskey
18–24 whole cloves
2 cups water

Preheat the oven to 400°F. Use a sharp boning or chef's knife to make parallel cuts ½ inch deep and ½ inch apart all over the ham, then give it a quarter-turn and repeat to produce a diamondlike appearance. Mix the sugar, mustard, and bourbon into a paste and rub it all over the top of the ham. Stick a clove in the center of each of the diamonds. Set the ham on a rack in a roasting pan and add the water.

Bake, uncovered, until an instant-read thermometer registers 130°F, about 90 minutes. During roasting, baste the ham at least twice, removing it from the oven and closing the oven door while basting to avoid losing oven heat.

Use a very sharp carving knife to cut thin slices and serve 2 to 3 slices per plate. Pour the basting liquid into a gravy boat and serve as a sauce for the ham. Wrap and refrigerate the remaining ham for up to 6 days. Freeze in freezer bags any ham that is not used the following week.

Sweet Potato Sauté

Serves 4, with 4 cups reserved for Ham, Sweet Potato, and Swiss Chard Frittata (page 115) and Ham, Shrimp, and Sweet Potato Jambalaya (page 113)

A simple preparation flavored with fresh thyme and parsley. These sweet potatoes beautifully complement the glazed ham and Swiss chard.

3 pounds sweet potatoes
5 tablespoons unsalted butter
1 small yellow onion (about 5 ounces), diced
1½ tablespoons minced fresh thyme
⅓ cup minced fresh parsley
Salt and freshly ground pepper to taste

Trim the ends of the sweet potatoes, but do not peel. Put the potatoes in a large pot, cover them with cold water, cover the pot, and bring the water to a boil. Uncover and reduce heat so the water boils gently. Cook until the potatoes are tender when pierced with a fork, about 15 minutes. Drain the potatoes and run them under cold water until cool enough to handle. Peel the potatoes and cut them into ½-inch dice. Set aside until ready to sauté.

About 15 minutes before serving, melt the butter in a 12-inch sauté pan or skillet over medium-high heat. Add the onion and sauté for 2 minutes. Add the cubed sweet potatoes and sauté until lightly browned. Reduce heat if the onions are browning too fast. Cook the sweet potatoes, stirring occasionally until browned, about 10 minutes. Stir in the thyme and parsley. Season with salt and pepper.

Set aside 4 cups of sweet potatoes to cool, and serve the rest. Cover and refrigerate the reserved sweet potatoes for up to 4 days.

Sautéed Swiss Chard

Serves 4, with 1¾ cups reserved for Ham, Sweet Potato, and Swiss Chard Frittata (page 115)

Swiss chard has dark green leaves with a firm white or red stalk. It is often overlooked, which is a shame, because it has a hearty, spinachlike taste with the addition of a crunchy stalk. It's a perfect accompaniment to ham.

4 bunches (2 to 2¼ pounds) Swiss chard
2 tablespoons unsalted butter
1 tablespoon olive oil
1 large garlic clove, minced
⅓ cup water
  Salt to taste

Wash the chard well in cold water, checking for any grit in its folds. Trim the end of the chard stalks and discard, then cut the stalks away from the leaves, reserving both. Cut the leaves into wide ribbons and pat them dry with paper towels or use a salad spinner. Set aside in a bowl. Cut the stems into 1-inch-wide strips, dry, and reserve in a separate bowl.

In a 6-inch skillet melt the butter over medium heat and cook until it foams and turns light brown but is not burnt. Remove from heat and set aside.

Ten minutes before serving, heat a 12-inch sauté pan or skillet over medium-high heat. Heat the olive oil and sauté the garlic until it begins to brown. Add the chard stems and sauté for 2 minutes. Add half the leaves and the water, stir to wilt the leaves, then add the remaining chard. Stir briefly, cover, and cook for 3 minutes. Remove the lid and stir in the browned butter and salt.

Set aside 1¼ cups chard to cool and serve the rest. Cover and refrigerate the reserved chard for up to 4 days.

Cherry Pie

Makes 8 to 10 servings

As we pointed out in The Basic Gourmet Entertains, *making a pie from scratch is a rewarding experience. Good homemade pies are usually better than any you can buy, and not particularly difficult to do once you've decided to learn to make one.*

CRUST:

2½ cups all-purpose flour

1 teaspoon salt

2 tablespoons granulated sugar

½ cup (1 stick) plus 3 tablespoons very cold unsalted butter, cut into tablespoon-sized portions

7 tablespoons very cold solid vegetable shortening

6–8 tablespoons very cold water

TO MAKE THE CRUST: Combine the dry ingredients in a food processor fitted with the metal blade. Add the butter and shortening and pulse until the butter pieces are the size of peas. Add 6 tablespoons of the water and process for a few seconds, just until a ball of dough begins to form. Add more water, 1 tablespoon at a time if needed to form the dough into a mass. Do not process after the dough ball forms. (To make the dough by hand, use two knives or a pastry blade to cut the butter and shortening into the dry ingredients, and a fork or your fingers to mix in the liquids and gently form a mass.)

Transfer the dough to a floured work surface, gathering all the loose bits, and form into a ball. Cut the dough into 2 pieces, one slightly larger than the other. Form each piece into a ball, flatten to about 1 inch thick, enclose in plastic wrap, and refrigerate for at least 30 minutes or as long as overnight.

continued on page 111

FILLING:

3 cans (16 ounces *each*) tart red pie
    cherries packed in water
1¼ cups granulated sugar
    Pinch of salt
¼ teaspoon red food coloring (optional)
¼ teaspoon almond extract
2½ teaspoons vanilla extract
5 tablespoons quick-cooking tapioca

1 tablespoon cold unsalted butter, cut into
    pea-sized bits
1 tablespoon milk
1 tablespoon turbinado sugar (see Cook's
    Note) or granulated sugar

TO MAKE THE FILLING: Drain the cherries in a strainer set over a medium bowl. Pour the juice into a glass measure up to the ¾-cup mark, then discard the remaining juice. Place the reserved juice back in the bowl along with the sugar, salt, optional food coloring, almond extract, vanilla, and tapioca. Stir to combine thoroughly, then add the cherries and stir again.

Preheat the oven to 400°F. Select a 9- to 10-inch pie plate. On a lightly floured work surface, roll the smaller piece of dough out to a circle about 12 inches in diameter. Dust the work surface and dough with a little more flour as necessary to keep the dough from sticking. The dough will be very delicate, and its edges will not be perfectly smooth. Roll the dough circle around the rolling pin, lift it over the pie plate, and unroll the dough over the plate, allowing it to settle into the plate. Moisten the dough with a little cold water to patch any holes or cracks.

Pour the filling into the crust. Sprinkle the butter bits over the filling. Roll out the remaining dough. Moisten the exposed part of the filled crust with a pastry brush dipped in water, or your wet finger. Drape the top crust over the pie. Press the top and bottom crust edges together with your fingers or a fork. Trim the excess dough by running a knife around the edge of the pan. Cut 5 or 6 slits in the top crust. Brush with the milk and sprinkle the sugar over.

Place the pie on a baking pan (nonstick if possible) to catch drips and bake for 20 minutes. Reduce heat to 350°F and bake until the crust is golden brown, about 40 more minutes. Let cool for several hours before slicing. Cut into 8 or 10 pieces. Cover leftover pie with plastic wrap and refrigerate for up to 7 days.

COOK'S NOTE   *Turbinado sugar can be found in the baking supplies aisle in some supermarkets. It is very light brown, has large crystals, and sprinkles easily.*

Cheddar Macaroni with Ham

Serves 4, with 4 servings left over

Nearly everyone has childhood memories of one of the all-time comfort foods, macaroni and cheese. If you are lucky, your memories are of the real McCoy, not something popped in a microwave oven or "made" from the fixings in a blue box. What follows is simple: a homemade cheese sauce poured over barely cooked elbow macaroni with diced ham and topped with buttered bread crumbs. Chilled leftovers can easily be cut into serving portions and frozen.

9 tablespoons unsalted butter
5 tablespoons all-purpose flour
3¼ cups whole milk
½ teaspoon salt
1 teaspoon dry mustard
½ teaspoon hot pepper sauce
5 cups (12 ounces) shredded extra-sharp Cheddar cheese
12 ounces small elbow macaroni
3 cups ½-inch dice Bourbon-Glazed Ham (page 106)
3 cups fresh bread crumbs, or an 8-ounce baguette (about 16 inches long), torn to pieces and ground in a food processor or blender

Preheat the oven to 350°F. Grease a 9-by-13-inch baking dish. In a 4-quart saucepan, melt 5 tablespoons of the butter over medium heat. Stir in the flour. Cook, stirring, until the mixture is very lightly browned. Gradually whisk in the milk, about 1 cup at a time. Add the salt, mustard, and hot pepper sauce. Bring to a simmer, whisking frequently, and cook for 5 minutes. Add the cheese and cook until it melts. Turn off heat.

Bring a 4-quart or larger pot of water to a rolling boil. Add the macaroni and cook, stirring occasionally, until it is al dente (cooked through but still quite chewy), about 6 minutes. Do not overcook; the noodles will continue to cook while baking. Drain in a colander, shaking out as much water as possible. Mix the noodles with the ham and spread in the prepared dish. Pour the sauce over. Melt the remaining 4 tablespoons butter and mix into the bread crumbs. Spread the crumb topping over the macaroni. Bake until bubbly, about 30 minutes. If the crumbs have not browned handsomely, place the casserole under the broiler for a few seconds before serving.

Serve half of the macaroni and cheese and set aside the rest to cool. Cover and refrigerate the reserved macaroni and cheese for up to 5 days. To freeze, cut into servings, wrap individually, and freeze for up to 3 months.

Ham, Shrimp, and Sweet Potato Jambalaya

Serves 4

Louisiana, home to French-influenced Creole and Cajun cooking, is also home to jambalaya, a rice dish made with the fruits of the land and waters. One of the most famous jambalayas combines shrimp and ham. This version adds the sweetness and color of sweet potatoes. It calls for short-grain rice, sometimes labeled California Pearl.

1 cup water

½ teaspoon salt

¼ cup short-grain white rice

3 tablespoons unsalted butter

2 large garlic cloves, minced

1 medium onion (6 to 8 ounces), chopped

¼ green bell pepper, seeded, deribbed, and finely chopped

1 can (14 ounces) crushed or diced tomatoes in juice or purée

Pinch of ground cloves

¼ teaspoon dried thyme

¼ teaspoon cayenne pepper

¼ cup minced fresh parsley

2½ cups (¾ pound) ½-inch dice Bourbon-Glazed Ham (page 106)

8 ounces bay (tiny cooked) shrimp

2 cups Sweet Potato Sauté (page 107)

In a 1-quart saucepan, bring the water to a boil. Add the salt and rice, cover, and cook over very low heat for 20 minutes. Fluff the rice with a fork and set aside, uncovered.

In a 10-inch skillet, melt the butter over medium heat and sauté the garlic, onion, and green pepper until soft but not browned, about 5 minutes. Set aside.

In a 2-quart or larger nonreactive saucepan, combine the tomatoes and juice, cloves, thyme, cayenne, and parsley. Cook over medium-high heat, regulating the heat so the mixture simmers briskly, until it is slightly thickened, about 8 minutes.

Return the skillet to medium-low heat. Add the ham, shrimp, sweet potatoes, rice, and tomato mixture to the pepper mixture, and stir to combine. Cover and heat over medium-low heat. Serve in bowls.

Asian Noodle Bowl with Ham

Serves 4

To make this quick soup, explore the Asian-foods section of a well-stocked supermarket. We used rice noodles rather than wheat or egg noodles in this recipe because they need only be soaked in warm water.

4 ounces rice stick noodles (see Cook's Note)

10 dried black (shiitake) mushrooms

8 cups Chicken Stock (page 23) or canned low-salt chicken broth

3 slices fresh ginger (about the size of a quarter), peeled and minced

1 large carrot, peeled and cut on the diagonal into ⅛-inch-thick ovals

1 tablespoon low-salt soy sauce

1½ cups julienned Bourbon-Glazed Ham (page 106)

1 bunch fresh watercress, cut into 2-inch lengths

2 green onions, including green tops, cut into 1-inch lengths

Place the rice noodles in a large bowl, cover with warm water, and soak for 20 minutes. Drain in a colander and set aside. Place the dried mushrooms in a small container with a tight-fitting lid. Add warm water to the top, close the container, and soak for 15 minutes. (Dried mushrooms float; placing them in a covered container ensures they will be submerged.) Drain, pat dry with paper towels, trim off stems, and cut into thin strips.

Meanwhile, in a 3½- to 4-quart saucepan, bring the stock or broth to a boil. Reduce heat to a simmer, add the ginger and carrot, and cook until the carrot is crisp-tender, 12 to 15 minutes. Add the soy sauce, ham, watercress, green onions, drained rice noodles, and mushrooms. Stir to combine and heat through. Ladle into warm soup bowls and serve immediately.

COOK'S NOTE *Rice stick noodles are thin, dry white noodles made from rice flour. They are typically packaged in cellophane bags. The noodles are available in assorted widths, anywhere from ⅟₁₆- to ¼-inch wide; any width will work just fine for this recipe.*

Ham, Sweet Potato, and Swiss Chard Frittata

Serves 4 generously, or can be cut into 6 wedges to save 2 for a terrific lunch

Frittatas are a perfect way to use up leftovers while making a rather elegant dinner. Assemble some cubed ham, chard, and potatoes in a skillet, pour beaten eggs over them, cook for a few minutes, brown under the broiler, and dinner is ready. All you need is some crusty bread and a simple salad, if you like, to round out this meal.

10 large eggs
¼ cup milk
¼ teaspoon salt
  Freshly ground pepper to taste
3 tablespoons olive oil
2 cups Sweet Potato Sauté (page 107)
2 cups ½-inch dice Bourbon-Glazed
  Ham (page 106)
1¼ cups Sautéed Swiss Chard (page 108)
¼ cup grated Parmesan cheese

Crack the eggs into a large bowl; using a fork, beat with the milk, salt, and pepper just until blended.

Preheat the broiler. In a 12-inch (preferably nonstick) ovenproof skillet over medium-high heat, heat the olive oil. Add the potatoes and ham and sauté until heated through, about 2 minutes. Add the chard and sauté to heat through. Turn heat to medium low and pour the egg mixture into the pan. Cook without covering or stirring until the egg mixture is almost set on top (it should quiver a little when you shake the pan). Sprinkle the Parmesan evenly over the top, then place the pan under the broiler until the frittata browns. Remove the pan from the broiler, let stand for 1 or 2 minutes, cut into wedges, and serve immediately.

weekend

GRILLED CHICKEN WITH HERBED MUSTARD
GRILLED CORN ON THE COB
GRILLED ZUCCHINI AND SUMMER SQUASH
FOCACCIA
ICE CREAM WITH RASPBERRY SAUCE AND
SLICED PEACHES

monday

SPICY CORN CHOWDER
Leftover grilled chicken and corn are
the basis for a fabulous soup that packs
jalapeño punch.

wednesday

**CHICKEN QUESADILLAS WITH
TOMATILLO SALSA**
Use the rest of the chicken to make
some super fast quesadillas. It takes
about 5 minutes to put together a fresh
salsa using tangy tomatillos.

thursday

**FOCACCIA SANDWICH WITH GRILLED
SQUASH, GOAT CHEESE, AND BASIL**
Focaccia becomes a centerpiece when
combined with leftover grilled squash.
This vegetarian dinner comes together
amazingly fast with the addition of goat
cheese, pesto, and some fresh basil.

The flavor of simple grilled chicken is incomparable, but we include directions for alternate cooking methods for those who do not own a grill. Accompany the chicken with some fine grilled or roasted corn on the cob and grilled or broiled summer squash. The recipe for focaccia is fun and simple. Finish the meal with the delights of summer: vanilla ice cream topped with sliced fresh peaches and raspberry purée.

Start the focaccia early on the day of serving, since it needs to rise twice. The raspberry purée can also be made early in the day. Everything else happens quickly once the grill has heated. First, grill the corn and keep it warm while grilling the chicken, and then finish in a flash with the squash.

Plenty of food will be left over for some delicious dinners during the week. The grilled chicken is used both in quesadillas and a charming soup. The remaining focaccia becomes a vegetarian sandwich.

Grilled Chicken with Herbed Mustard

Makes 2 chickens, 1 to serve (for 4 people) and 1 to reserve for Spicy Corn Chowder (page 125) and Chicken Quesadillas with Tomatillo Salsa (page 126)

Chicken is relatively easy to grill and leaves the happy cook with fully flavored leftovers that can be used in creative ways. Broiling can accomplish much the same look and texture.

2 whole chickens, about 3½ pounds each
2 tablespoons Dijon-style mustard
1 teaspoon hot pepper sauce
2 tablespoons olive oil
2 tablespoons Worcestershire sauce
2 cups lightly packed fresh parsley leaves, minced
½ teaspoon ground pepper

Prepare a medium-hot fire in a kettle-style charcoal grill or preheat a gas or electric grill. Butterfly the chickens by setting them, breast-side down, on a cutting board. Use a pair of poultry shears, kitchen scissors, or a sharp chef's knife to cut through the chickens from one end to the other on each side of the backbones to remove them. Save the backbones (and any gizzards, hearts, and necks) to freeze for making stock. Spread the chickens out, skin-side up, and press down firmly to flatten them. Use your fingers and a paper towel to pull the skin off the birds, excepting the wings. If both birds will not fit at once on your grill, cut off the wings and leg-thigh sections so you can fit all the pieces on.

In a small bowl, whisk the mustard, pepper sauce, olive oil, Worcestershire sauce, parsley, and pepper together. Use your fingers to spread this mixture evenly over both sides of the chickens. Place the chickens on the grill, cover the grill, partially close the top vents so the fire stays medium-hot, and cook for about 13 minutes. Turn, cover, and cook until an instant-read thermometer registers at least 170°F when inserted in the thickest portion of the thigh without touching bone.

Set aside 1 chicken to cool completely. Let the remaining chicken rest for 5 minutes before cutting up and serving. Wrap and refrigerate the reserved chicken for up to 7 days.

COOK'S NOTE   *To broil, preheat the broiler. Place 1 chicken on a broiler pan lined with aluminum foil and place it about 6 inches below the heat source. Broil on one side until lightly browned, about 15 minutes. Turn and broil the other side until lightly brown, about 15 minutes. Test as above. Lower the rack if the chicken needs more time to cook but is browning too quickly. Repeat to cook the second bird.*

Grilled Corn on the Cob

Serves 4 (1 ear each), with 4 ears reserved for Spicy Corn Chowder (page 125)

When local fresh corn appears in the market, we can't wait to cook it. If you have never grilled corn, by all means try this recipe.

8 fresh ears of corn
4 tablespoons (½ stick) unsalted butter, melted
Salt and freshly ground pepper to taste

Prepare the grill and have the coals hot. Pull down the husk from each ear of corn, remove the silk, then replace the husks. Run water into the corn, drain the excess, then twist the husk closed at the top.

Grill for 20 minutes, turning several times to grill all sides. When ready to serve, pull off the husks, brush the corn with melted butter, and season with salt and pepper. Set aside 4 ears of corn to cool and serve the rest. Wrap the reserved corn and store in the refrigerator for up to 4 days.

COOK'S NOTE   *An alternative cooking method is to follow the same preparation steps, then roast the corn in a preheated 475°F oven for 20 minutes.*

Grilled Zucchini and Summer Squash

Serves 4, with 1½ cups reserved for Focaccia Sandwich with Grilled Squash, Goat Cheese, and Basil (page 127)

There is nothing like grilled vegetables in the summer, and they make terrific leftovers.

3 medium zucchini (about 1¼ pounds)
3 medium summer squash (about 1½ pounds)
¼ cup olive oil
Salt and freshly ground pepper to taste

Prepare the grill and have the coals hot. Slice off the stem end of the zucchini and squash and discard. Slice on the diagonal into ¼-inch-thick ovals. Lay the slices in a single layer on a pan or baking sheet. Use the ¼ cup olive oil to brush each slice on both sides. Sprinkle salt and pepper on the top side of each slice. Place on the grill in a single layer. Cook on one side until nicely browned, about 3 minutes. Turn and cook on the other side for 2 to 3 minutes. Alternatively, leave the slices on the baking sheet and broil until nicely browned on both sides.

PESTO OIL:
3 tablespoons olive oil
3 tablespoons Pesto (recipe follows; see Cook's Note)

TO MAKE THE PESTO OIL: Mix the olive oil with the pesto. Blend well. Reserve 2 tablespoons for leftovers.

Brush the remaining pesto oil on one side of the grilled zucchini and squash when ready to serve.

Set aside 1½ cups vegetables to cool and serve the rest. Cover and store in the refrigerator for up to 4 days.

Pesto
2 cups fresh basil leaves
½ cup good-quality olive oil
4 garlic cloves, minced
1 teaspoon salt
½ cup (2 ounces) freshly grated Parmesan cheese

Combine the basil, olive oil, garlic, and salt in a blender or food processor. Blend until smooth. Add the Parmesan and blend just to combine. Store the pesto in a covered jar in the refrigerator for up to 2 weeks, or freeze it for up to 6 months. Makes about 1 cup.

COOK'S NOTE   *You can use a store-bought pesto for this recipe; we always keep some in the freezer. However, an easy pesto recipe is given in case you want to make your own.*

Focaccia

Makes 1 ten-inch round loaf to serve, and 1 to freeze for Focaccia Sandwich with Grilled Squash, Goat Cheese, and Basil (page 127)

Focaccia dough is pliable, easy, and fun to work with. It's a grown-up's Play-Doh. This recipe produces 2 soft, delicious focaccias luxuriantly drizzled with olive oil. We serve one with our grilled chicken dinner, and freeze the other for a luscious vegetarian sandwich later in the week. Fresh sage is used in this version, but almost any fresh herb is wonderful—try basil, oregano, or rosemary. We encourage the use of coarse salt for the topping; if available, coarse sea salt is especially aromatic.

1 package (2½ teaspoons) active dry yeast
¼ cup warm water (105° to 115°F)
2 cups lukewarm water (about 85°F)
2 tablespoons extra-virgin olive oil
5½–6 cups all-purpose flour
2 teaspoons salt

Combine the yeast and warm water in a large bowl. Stir and let sit for 5 minutes or until foamy. Stir in the lukewarm water, salt, and olive oil. Add 4 cups of the flour and stir well with a wooden spoon. Stir in enough of the additional flour to make a lightly sticky dough and turn the dough out on a floured work surface. Knead the dough, adding sprinkles of flour as needed to prevent sticking, until smooth, elastic, and slightly sticky, about 5 minutes. Put the dough in a large oiled bowl, turn the dough to coat it with oil, and cover with plastic wrap. Let rise at room temperature until doubled in bulk, 1 to 2 hours.

Oil two 10-inch cake pans with olive oil. Turn the dough out onto a floured work surface. Divide the dough in half and knead each half briefly. Place each half in an oiled pan. Press the dough down to cover the bottom of the pans. Let the dough relax for several minutes if it resists being spread. Cover each pan with plastic wrap and let the dough rise again until soft and fluffy but not quite doubled in bulk, about 1 hour. The dough can also be refrigerated at this time for several hours or overnight before proceeding. Remove from the refrigerator 1½ to 2 hours before baking to let rise.

¼ cup coarsely chopped fresh sage
2 tablespoons extra-virgin olive oil
2 generous teaspoons coarse salt

About 30 minutes before baking, preheat the oven to 400°F. Make random light indentations in each piece of dough with your fingertips. Sprinkle each with the sage, drizzle with the olive oil, and sprinkle with the coarse salt. Place the pans in the oven and spray the walls of the oven with water from a spray bottle (see Cook's Note). Spray again after 4 minutes, then again after 8 minutes. After 10 minutes, reduce the oven temperature to 375°F and bake until golden brown, another 20 to 25 minutes.

COOK'S NOTE   *Baking yeast breads while there is steam in the oven allows them to rise higher before a crust forms and helps create a chewier crust. An easy way to produce steam in an oven is to mist it with a few sprays of tap water from a clean spray bottle during the first few minutes of baking.*

Ice Cream with Raspberry Sauce and Sliced Peaches

Serves 4

This grill menu is not particularly rich, even though it is filled with bold flavors. It would be wonderful followed by a creamy and fruity dessert, such as this combination of fresh peaches and raspberries with vanilla ice cream. If fresh raspberries are out of season, use a small package of thawed unsweetened frozen berries.

1 cup (½ pint) fresh raspberries
2 tablespoons sugar
2 ripe peaches, peeled and pitted
1 pint quality vanilla ice cream, such as
   Häagen-Dazs or Breyer's

In a blender or food processor, purée the raspberries and sugar until smooth. Strain through a fine-meshed sieve to remove the seeds. Cut each peach into 8 slices.

Place 2 scoops ice cream in each of 4 dessert bowls. Spoon the raspberry sauce around the base of the ice cream and arrange 4 peach slices around the ice cream. Serve.

Spicy Corn Chowder

Serves 4

A real meal in a bowl, this satisfying soup incorporates bright chili and lime flavors as well as the pungency of cilantro. Hot liquid is ladled over the vegetables to preserve their fresh texture, so be sure to heat the serving bowls to make sure the chowder is hot enough.

2 tablespoons vegetable oil

1 large onion (10 to 12 ounces), coarsely chopped

2 garlic cloves, crushed

2–3 large (2 pounds) russet potatoes, peeled, halved, and each half cut into 8 pieces

1 jalapeño chili, halved, and one half seeded and minced

5 cups Chicken Stock (page 23), or canned low-salt broth

Salt and freshly ground pepper to taste

2–3 cups thinly sliced Grilled Chicken with Herbed Mustard (page 119)

Kernels cut from 4 ears of Grilled Corn on the Cob (1½ to 2½ cups; page 120)

4 slices bacon, cooked crisp and crumbled, or 1½ cups chopped smoked almonds

½ cup lightly packed parsley leaves, minced

1 cup lightly packed cilantro leaves, minced

4 green onions, thinly sliced

4 Roma (plum) tomatoes, each cut into 8 wedges

1 lime, cut into 4 wedges

In a 4-quart or larger saucepan over medium heat, heat the oil. Add the onion and garlic and sauté until vegetables are soft but not browned, about 5 minutes. Add the potatoes, the half chili with seeds, and stock. Bring the mixture to a boil over medium-high heat, reduce heat to a simmer, cover, and cook for 15 minutes. Pour the liquid through a large strainer into a medium bowl. In a blender or food processor, purée the solids, adding liquid as necessary to assist the machine. Return the puréed soup and any remaining liquid to the pan and add salt and pepper to taste. Keep the liquid at a simmer while finishing the soup.

Preheat the oven to 200°F. Heat 4 heavy soup bowls in the oven for 10 minutes. In a medium bowl toss the chicken, corn, bacon, parsley, cilantro, green onions, and minced chili. Arrange 8 tomato wedges in bottom of each heated bowl. Divide the tossed ingredients equally among the bowls. Ladle the hot soup equally into each bowl. Serve immediately, with a wedge of lime for each diner.

Chicken Quesadillas with Tomatillo Salsa

Serves 4

Here is a terrific way to use extra grilled chicken. Your family won't even know this is a "leftover" meal.

TOMATILLO SALSA:

- 1 can (12 ounces) whole tomatillos, drained and diced
- 1 tablespoon fresh lime juice
- 2 tablespoons minced fresh Anaheim chili (see Cook's Notes)
- 1 serrano chili, seeded and minced (see Cook's Notes)
- ¼ teaspoon salt
- ¼ teaspoon granulated sugar
- 3 tablespoons fresh cilantro leaves

- 6 flour tortillas, 10 inches in diameter
- 1 cup (4 ounces) shredded pepper jack cheese
- 1 thigh and 1 half-breast Grilled Chicken with Herbed Mustard (page 119), shredded (1½ cups)

TO MAKE THE SALSA: Put the tomatillos in a small bowl and stir in all the remaining salsa ingredients. Taste and adjust the seasoning. Set aside until ready to serve.

Heat a heavy 12-inch skillet over high heat. Place a tortilla in the pan and sprinkle with one third of the cheese and one third of the chicken. Cover with a second tortilla. When the bottom tortilla is nicely browned, use a wide spatula to turn the quesadilla. Brown the other side. Place on a cutting board. Repeat to cook the other 2 quesadillas. Use a sharp knife or a pizza cutter to cut each quesadilla into 6 wedges. Arrange the wedges on a warm platter and serve immediately. Pass the salsa to spoon on top of the quesadillas.

COOK'S NOTES *We recommend keeping some disposable surgical gloves on hand (available at any pharmacy) to wear while working with fresh chilies. Oils from cut fresh chilies on your hands can easily irritate your eyes or nose if touched.*

Anaheim chilies are large, long green fresh chilies that are mild in flavor. Serrano chilies are small, green, hot fresh chilies. Serranos are hotter than jalapeños and a little smaller. Look for these chilies in the produce aisle of a well-stocked supermarket.

Focaccia Sandwich with Grilled Squash, Goat Cheese, and Basil

Serves 4

This dinner is for frazzled days! In 30 minutes, dinner is served using the delicious leftovers from the weekend menu. You merely warm the focaccia and squash, and assemble the sandwich. The sandwich is subject to all kinds of variations of cheeses and vegetables.

1 frozen 10-inch Focaccia (page 122)
1½ cups Grilled Zucchini and Summer Squash (page 121)
2 tablespoons Pesto Oil (page 121)
5 ounces fresh white goat cheese
½ cup loosely packed fresh basil leaves

Place the frozen focaccia, unwrapped, in the oven. Turn the oven to 300°F. Heat for 20 to 30 minutes. Meanwhile, place the grilled squash in a baking dish and warm it in the oven along with the focaccia. When the bread has defrosted all the way through and is slightly warm, remove it from the oven and slice it in half horizontally. Place the top back in the turned-off oven to keep warm while assembling the rest of the sandwich.

Spread the pesto oil on the bottom of the focaccia. Top with the warm squash. Crumble the goat cheese over the squash. If the basil leaves are large, tear them in half and then sprinkle them on top of the sandwich. Cover with the warm top, cut into wedges with a serrated knife, and serve immediately.

COOK'S NOTE *Don't worry about exact amounts. A little more or less goat cheese or vegetables is fine.*

weekend

GRILLED BUTTERFLIED LEG OF LAMB
YOGURT, GOAT CHEESE, AND SUN-DRIED
TOMATO SPREAD
GRILLED EGGPLANT AND ONION SLICES
PITA BREADS
NECTARINE AND BLUEBERRY CRISP

monday

LAMB CURRY
Thai-inspired seasonings make a wonderful
curry sauce to which cooked lamb is
added at the very last minute and served
over a mound of rice.

tuesday

**LAMB AND PITA SANDWICHES WITH
YOGURT-MINT SAUCE**
Leftover lamb is sliced thin for this
supper, stuffed in leftover split pitas
with chopped lettuce and drizzled with
a fresh yogurt-mint sauce.

wednesday

**PENNE WITH GRILLED VEGETABLES
AND SUN-DRIED TOMATO SAUCE**
The remaining yogurt–goat cheese spread
becomes a sauce for a vegetarian pasta
dish that includes the coarsely chopped
grilled eggplant and onion slices.

thursday

LAMB AND TOMATO DOUBLE-CRUST PIZZA
A quick-rise pizza dough makes a
kid-pleasing "stuffed" pizza using diced
leftover lamb, some thin-sliced fresh
plum tomatoes, and a blend of cheeses.

Here is a wonderful summer menu, easy and relaxed, featuring a gorgeous butterflied leg of lamb. Thick slices of eggplant and onion are also cooked on the grill. Don't worry if you don't have a grill. We give directions for alternative cooking methods. The menu starts with a simple appetizer. We also give a recipe for pita breads, which are really very easy.

On the morning of the day of serving, set the yogurt for the Yogurt, Goat Cheese, and Sun-Dried Tomato Spread to drain. You will then be ready to blend it after six or eight hours. You can also make the crisp the morning of serving and leave it at room temperature. About 2 hours before serving, marinate the lamb and then make the pita bread dough. While the pita dough is resting, grill the vegetables, then set them aside covered with aluminum foil. When the vegetables are done, put the lamb on the grill and cook the pitas. Rewarm the vegetables briefly after the pitas are done.

A leg of lamb provides generous leftovers for three more dinners. The yogurt—goat cheese spread also provides the basis for a great vegetarian pasta.

Grilled Butterflied Leg of Lamb

Serves 4, with 2 cups diced lamb reserved for Lamb and Pita Sandwiches with Yogurt-Mint Sauce (page 138), 3 cups sliced for Lamb Curry (page 137), and 1 cup diced for Lamb and Roma Tomato Double-Crust Pizza (page 140)

Lamb is a wonderfully versatile meat found in most supermarkets, both bone-in and boneless. You may find a butterflied leg of lamb ready to purchase in your market. If not, look for a boneless leg of lamb roast, usually sold netted and inside a plastic package. Or, ask the store's butcher to bone and butterfly (spread out flat) a leg for you. Served here with a variety of grilled vegetables and hot-out-of-the-oven pita bread, leg of lamb is a robust treat. The leftover lamb will also be a treat a few days later.

---

1 boned and butterflied leg of lamb, 4 to 5 pounds

Leaves from 2 sprigs (about 6 inches each) fresh rosemary, minced, or 2 teaspoons dried rosemary, crushed

1 tablespoon ground pepper

¾ teaspoon salt

Lay the butterflied lamb leg on a cutting board, skin-side up. (If you purchased a rolled and tied boneless roast, cut off the string or netting and open the roast flat.) Use a sharp chef's knife or boning knife to remove any skin and fat. Mix the rosemary, pepper, and salt together. Rub the seasonings into both sides of the meat, wrap the meat in plastic, and refrigerate for 1 to 2 hours.

Light a hot fire in a charcoal grill or preheat a gas or electric grill (pages 12–13). Remove the lamb from the refrigerator 30 minutes before grilling and unwrap. Grill or broil the lamb until medium-rare, when an instant-read thermometer inserted in the thickest part of the meat registers 120° to 130°F, about 10 minutes per side. Let rest for 5 minutes before carving about one-third of the lamb into thin slices across the grain. Cool, wrap, and refrigerate the remaining lamb for up to 5 days.

Yogurt, Goat Cheese, and Sun-Dried Tomato Spread

Serves 4, with 1½ cups reserved for Penne with Grilled Vegetables and Sun-Dried Tomato Sauce (page 139)

This flavorful spread uses yogurt cheese, or drained yogurt. Use a yogurt that does not contain gelatin. The spread is lower in fat than if it were all goat cheese, but it also has a great taste: tangy and creamy. Leftover spread becomes a dynamite sauce for pasta later in the week.

2 cups (1 pint) plain nonfat yogurt

5 ounces fresh white goat cheese at room temperature

4 ounces (½ cup) oil-packed sun-dried tomatoes, drained and chopped (see Cook's Notes)

2 tablespoons chopped fresh basil

¼ teaspoon salt

Freshly ground black pepper to taste

Dash of hot red pepper sauce (see Cook's Notes)

On the morning of the serving day, line a colander or sieve with a double layer of cheesecloth. Set it over a bowl and place the yogurt in the strainer. Let drain in the refrigerator for 6 to 8 hours. Discard the drippings.

When ready to make the spread, mash the goat cheese in a medium bowl with the back of a fork. Add the drained yogurt, tomatoes, basil, salt, pepper, and hot sauce. Mix well to blend. Refrigerate until 30 minutes before serving.

CROSTINI:

½ loaf baguette cut into ¼-inch-thick slices

¼ cup olive oil

TO MAKE THE CROSTINI: Preheat the oven to 325°F. Brush the bread slices lightly on one side with olive oil. Place on a baking sheet and bake for 10 minutes. Turn and bake until lightly toasted and crisp, about 10 more minutes. Let cool completely. Arrange on a platter, oiled-side up.

Reserve 1½ cups of the yogurt–goat cheese spread. Serve the rest of the spread in a bowl alongside the crostini. Wrap and refrigerate reserved spread for up to 7 days.

COOK'S NOTES   *Sun-dried tomatoes packed in olive oil are more flavorful for this dish, but dried ones may be substituted. Simply soak them in hot water for 30 minutes. Drain, pat with a paper towel, and chop.*

The most common hot red pepper sauce is Tabasco, but there are many other sprightly brands available. Our current favorite is Frank's Original Red Hot.

Grilled Eggplant and Onion Slices

Serves 4, with about 2 cups *each* chopped eggplant and onion reserved for Penne with Grilled Vegetables and Sun-Dried Tomato Sauce (page 139)

This is a simple and delicious way to prepare vegetables. The recipe requires at least two sessions at the grill for the vegetables, but they cook quickly and will provide you with plenty of tasty leftovers for pasta or sandwiches. The balsamic reduction sauce is optional, but it's easy and delicious, especially with the eggplant.

½ cup balsamic vinegar (optional)
3 pounds large, firm, unblemished eggplants, stemmed and peeled
½ cup olive oil or more
3 pounds yellow onions, cut into ¼-inch thick slices (see Cook's Note)
Salt and freshly ground pepper to taste

Place the vinegar, if using, in a small nonreactive saucepan. Bring to a boil over medium heat and regulate the heat so that it simmers briskly. Watch it carefully; do not let it boil away. When it has reduced by half remove from heat and set aside.

Prepare the grill and have the coals hot. Cut each eggplant crosswise into ½-inch-thick slices. Brush each side lightly with olive oil and sprinkle with salt and pepper. Place the slices on the grill. Cook, turning once, until each side is well grill-marked and tender but not mushy, 3 to 4 minutes per side. Remove from the grill and, while still warm, brush with the reduced balsamic if using.

Brush the onions with olive oil on each side and sprinkle with salt and pepper. Place on the grill and cook, turning once, until well marked on each side and tender, 5 to 6 minutes a side. Transfer to a serving platter.

Set aside about 2 cups of the eggplant and 2 cups of the onions to cool and serve the rest. Wrap and refrigerate the reserved vegetables for up to 7 days.

COOK'S NOTE   *If you can find Walla Walla, Vidalia, Cuernavaca, Peru, or Maui sweet onions, buy them. They take a little longer to cook because of their high water content, but they are the sweetest.*

Pita Breads

Using commercially made pitas is fine, but your own pita breads are no particular trick to make and are a real crowd-pleaser. They freeze well as long as other foods are not piled on top of them in the freezer.

1 cup warm water (105° to 115°F)
Pinch of granulated sugar
1 package (2½ teaspoons) active dry yeast
1 teaspoon salt
2 tablespoons olive oil
3 cups all-purpose flour

Put the water in a 2-cup glass measure or small bowl. Add the sugar and yeast, stirring just to mix. Let sit until foamy, about 5 minutes. Add the salt and olive oil and stir well.

To make the dough in a food processor, put the flour in the workbowl fitted with the dough blade. Stir the yeast mixture and, with the machine running, pour it through the feed tube as quickly as the flour will absorb it without making a sloshing sound. Allow a ball of dough to form and rotate for 60 seconds, adding flour 1 tablespoon at a time if the dough seems too sticky for the machine.

To make the dough by hand, place the yeast mixture in a large bowl. Gradually stir in the flour until a ball of slightly sticky dough forms. Turn the dough out on a lightly floured surface. Flatten the dough, fold it over on itself once, and knead by pressing down on the dough a few times using your knuckles or the base of your palm. Continue to knead for about 5 minutes, flouring the surface and dough only as necessary to prevent the dough from sticking, until the dough is smooth and elastic.

Put the dough in a large bowl and cover with plastic wrap. Let rise in a warm place for 30 to 45 minutes, or until the dough is about doubled in size. (The dough may be refrigerated for several days at this point by placing it in a gallon-size plastic bag, squeezing the air out, and securing a twist tie at the top of the bag so the dough has room to expand; bring to room temperature before forming and baking.)

To bake, preheat the oven to 450°F. Position an oven rack at the center of the oven. Sprinkle 2 heavy or doubled baking sheets with cornmeal or line them with parchment paper.

Turn the dough out on a lightly floured surface. Using your hands, roll the dough into an even rope shape about 12 inches long. Cut the dough into 8 equal pieces. Form each piece into a ball and let rest for 5 minutes covered with a kitchen towel. Using a rolling pin, roll out each piece of dough into a circle about 6 inches in diameter and about ¼ inch thick. Place circles on each prepared pan. Let rest for 5 minutes. Place one pan in the oven and bake for about 4 minutes, or until the pitas have puffed up and browned just slightly. Remove the pan and bake the second pan of pitas.

Set aside 4 pitas to cool and serve the others, or stack the pitas to be served and wrap them in a kitchen towel to keep them warm.

Place the cooled reserved pitas in a gallon-size lock-top plastic bag and store in the freezer where they won't be damaged. Reheat on a baking sheet in a pre-heated 325°F oven for 20 minutes.

COOK'S NOTE   *1 cup whole-wheat flour may be substituted for 1 cup all-purpose flour; the dough will be slightly stickier.*

Nectarine and Blueberry Crisp

Serves 4, with half reserved for a weeknight dessert

Fruit crisps are a favorite summer dessert. We follow the season and combine whatever tastes best: strawberries and rhubarb; apricots, peaches, and cherries; plums, nectarines, and berries; and as the soft summer fruits wane, apples and pears. Serve crisps warm, accompanied with ice cream, sweetened whipped cream, or frozen yogurt.

TOPPING:

- ½ cup (2 ounces) walnuts, finely chopped
- ½ cup old-fashioned oats
- 1 cup all-purpose flour
- ½ cup packed light brown sugar
- 1 teaspoon ground cinnamon
- ½ teaspoon freshly grated nutmeg
- 6 tablespoons cold unsalted butter, cut into small pieces

TO MAKE THE TOPPING: Preheat the oven to 350°F. Spread the walnuts on a baking sheet and toast for 5 minutes, or until lightly browned and crisp. Let cool.

Meanwhile, in a medium bowl, combine the oats, flour, brown sugar, cinnamon, and nutmeg. Scatter the butter over the flour mixture. Blend the butter into the flour mixture with a pastry cutter or your fingertips until the mixture is crumbly. Add the walnuts and set aside.

FILLING:

- 10 nectarines (3 to 3½ pounds), peeled, pitted, and cut into eighths
- 2 cups (1 pint) fresh blueberries
- 2 tablespoons cornstarch
- ¼ cup orange juice
- ⅔ cup packed light brown sugar

TO MAKE THE FILLING: In a large bowl, combine the nectarines and blueberries. Gently mix. In a small bowl, blend the cornstarch, orange juice, and brown sugar until the cornstarch and sugar are dissolved. Add to the fruit and stir gently to blend. Spoon into a 9-by-13-inch glass or ceramic baking dish.

Sprinkle the topping evenly over the fruit. Bake until the crisp is nicely browned and the fruit is tender when pierced with a fork, 30 to 40 minutes. Serve half of the crisp warm or at room temperature, setting the other half aside to cool if necessary. Cover the reserved crisp and store at room temperature for up to 2 days.

COOK'S NOTES *Double or triple the topping, store it in the freezer, and you'll always be ready to put a crisp together. Use 8-ounce ovenproof ramekins to make individual fruit crisps.*

Lamb Curry

Serves 4

One of the most appealing ways to eat leftover lamb is in a simple curry sauce, served with a big mound of rice, Thai style. The primary seasonings are canned coconut milk and bottled curry paste, both available in the Asian foods section of many supermarkets. This is good eating, and not much work.

1 cup long-grain white rice

1½ cups water

½ teaspoon salt

2 tablespoons vegetable oil

2 quarter-size slices unpeeled fresh ginger, minced

1 jumbo yellow onion (14 to 16 ounces), diced

3 tablespoons red, green, or yellow Thai curry paste or to taste

3½ cups Chicken Stock (page 23) or canned low-salt chicken broth

1 can (about 14½ ounces) coconut milk

Freshly ground pepper to taste

6 tablespoons all-purpose flour

6 tablespoons cold water

2 limes, 1 juiced, the other cut into 4 wedges

1½ cups lightly packed fresh basil leaves, cut into thin shreds

1 apple (6 to 8 ounces), peeled, cored, and cut into ½-inch dice

3 cups 1-by-⅛-inch-sliced Grilled Butterflied Leg of Lamb (page 131)

In a 2-quart saucepan, combine the rice and water and bring to a boil over medium-high heat. Add the salt, reduce heat, cover, and cook at a bare simmer for 15 minutes without peeking or stirring. Remove from heat and let sit, covered, for up to 30 minutes.

In a 4-quart heavy saucepan over medium heat, heat the oil. Add the ginger and sauté for about 30 seconds. Add the onion and cook, stirring occasionally, until soft but not browned, about 5 minutes. Stir in the curry paste and cook for about 1 minute. Add the stock or broth and coconut milk, and grind in some pepper. Bring to a simmer. Place the flour and water in a small jar with a tight-fitting lid and shake vigorously to break up any lumps. Whisk into sauce, breaking up any lumps. Simmer for 5 minutes. Taste and adjust the seasoning.

When ready to serve, add the lime juice, basil, apple, and lamb to sauce. Ladle into wide soup plates or individual pasta bowls. Place a big mound of rice in the center of each bowl. Lay a lime wedge on top of rice. Serve.

Lamb and Pita Sandwiches with Yogurt-Mint Sauce

Serves 4

Here is a fun, casual sandwich supper from your lamb-dinner leftovers. Make a simple yogurt sauce, warm the pita breads, dice some lamb and veggies, and dinner is done. We add a little sour cream to our yogurt dip because we like the rich flavor it imparts, but if you are very fat-conscious, use all nonfat yogurt. The amount of lamb and veggies is approximate. Feel free to increase them for a hungry crowd.

YOGURT-MINT SAUCE:

1½ cups plain nonfat yogurt

½ cup sour cream

2 garlic cloves, minced

½ cup chopped fresh mint

¼ teaspoon salt

Freshly ground pepper to taste

2 dashes red pepper sauce

4 frozen Pita Breads (page 134) or purchased pitas

3 medium tomatoes (5 to 6 ounces *each*), sliced

2 tablespoons extra-virgin olive oil

1 tablespoon balsamic vinegar

Salt and freshly ground pepper to taste

2 cups diced Grilled Butterflied Leg of Lamb (page 131)

2 green onions, including green tops, thinly sliced

2 cups leaf lettuce, torn into bite-sized pieces

TO MAKE THE MINT SAUCE: In a medium bowl, combine all the sauce ingredients and stir to blend well. Refrigerate until ready to serve.

Preheat the oven to 325°F. Wrap the pita breads completely in a large piece of aluminum foil. Heat for 10 minutes if they are at room temperature, or 20 minutes if frozen.

In a large bowl, gently toss the tomato slices with the olive oil, vinegar, salt, and pepper. Place the lamb, green onions, tomatoes, lettuce, and sauce in separate bowls on the table. Remove the pitas from the oven and cut each in half. Give everyone 2 halves and let them fill their own pitas.

Penne with Grilled Vegetables and Sun-Dried Tomato Sauce

Serves 4

Two elements from your weekend dinner are incorporated into a great vegetarian weekday meal. The pasta will soak up a lot of sauce. If you don't have quite enough leftover spread, add a little milk to it. The tomato added at the end is not essential, but it adds a fresh note.

1 tablespoon salt

12 ounces penne

1½ cups Yogurt, Goat Cheese, and Sun-Dried Tomato Spread (page 132)

4 cups Grilled Eggplant and Onion (page 133), coarsely chopped

1 medium tomato (5 to 6 ounces), sliced into thin wedges

Bring 6 quarts of water to a boil in a large pot over high heat. Add the salt. Add the penne and cook, stirring often, until al dente (cooked through, but still slightly chewy), about 10 minutes.

While the pasta is cooking, warm the spread slightly in a microwave on medium power, or in a small saucepan over low heat.

Drain the pasta, return it to the pan, and toss with the spread, eggplant and onion, and tomato. Divide among 4 warm pasta bowls.

Lamb and Roma Tomato Double-Crust Pizza

Serves 4

Lamb is so flavorful that even little bits of it add flavor to salads, soups, hashes, casseroles, and so on. A pizza is also a tasty destination for leftover lamb, in this case in concert with Roma tomatoes, found in many markets year-round and usually with better flavor than other tomatoes. A little chopped rosemary continues the theme begun when grilling the lamb. And for variety's sake, the pizza is formed with a double crust and makes a handsome presentation. The dough may be made up to four days in advance and refrigerated, to make it easier to prepare the pizza during the week.

PIZZA DOUGH:

1 cup warm water (105° to 115°F)
  Pinch of sugar
1 package (2½ teaspoons) active dry yeast
½ teaspoon salt
3 tablespoons olive oil
2½ cups all-purpose flour
½ cup white or yellow cornmeal

In a small bowl or 2-cup measure, combine the water and sugar. Stir in the yeast and let stand until the mixture is bubbly. Whisk in the salt and olive oil.

TO MAKE THE DOUGH IN A FOOD PROCESSOR: Combine the flour and cornmeal in the workbowl fitted with the dough blade. Stir the liquid mixture and, with the machine running, pour the liquid into the flour mixture as fast as it will absorb it without making a sloshing sound (a sloshing sound means you are pouring too fast). Allow a dough ball to form and knead for 60 seconds, adding more flour only if the dough is so sticky that the processor is struggling. Add 1 tablespoon of water at a time if there are dry bits of dough loose in the machine. For the best results the dough should be slightly sticky.

TO MAKE THE DOUGH BY HAND: Place the yeast mixture in a large bowl. In another bowl, blend the flour and cornmeal with a whisk. Gradually stir the flour mixture into the yeast mixture until a ball of slightly sticky dough forms. Turn the dough out on a lightly floured surface. Flatten the dough, fold it over on itself once, and knead by pressing down on the dough a few times using your knuckles or the base of your palm. Continue to knead for about 5 minutes, flouring the surface and dough only as necessary to prevent the dough from sticking, until the dough is smooth and elastic.

2 tablespoons olive oil

1 tablespoon minced fresh rosemary

1 cup lightly packed fresh parsley leaves, coarsely chopped

3 Roma (plum) tomatoes, peeled, each cut into 6 slices

1 cup diced Grilled Butterflied Leg of Lamb (page 131)

1 cup (4 ounces) grated Parmesan cheese

2–3 cups (8 to 12 ounces) shredded jack, mozzarella, Gruyère, Emmenthaler, or Havarti cheese, or a mixture

Place the dough in a gallon-size plastic bag, squeeze the air out, and seal the bag at the *top* so that the dough has room to rise. Let rise in a warm place until doubled in size, 45 minutes or more depending on room temperature. To refrigerate for up to 4 days, open the bag, deflate the dough, return it to the bag as before, and refrigerate. Roll the refrigerated dough out while it is cold.

Preheat the oven to 450°F. Sprinkle a 12-inch ovenproof skillet or deep dish pizza pan with a little cornmeal to make the pizza easier to remove, or use a nonstick pan.

Cut the dough into 2 pieces, one slightly larger than the other. On a floured surface, roll the larger piece out to a diameter 2 inches wider than the pan. Dust the top with flour. Fold in half, then in half again so it looks like a pizza slice. Set in the pan as if it were a slice, and unfold. Adjust the dough so it is centered in the pan. Brush 1 tablespoon of the olive oil all over dough. Sprinkle the rosemary and parsley over. Arrange the tomato slices over the dough, spread the lamb pieces around, and top with the cheeses. Roll the remaining dough to the same size as the pan. Lay it on top of the pizza and crimp the dough edges together. Cut a couple of slits in the top and brush 1 tablespoon olive oil over top crust. Bake until the crust is handsomely browned, 12 to 15 minutes.

weekend

POACHED HALIBUT WITH CHIPOTLE SAUCE
STEAMED NEW POTATOES
STIR-FRIED BABY BOK CHOY
LEMON–POPPY SEED CAKE

monday

HALIBUT TACOS
Leftover chipotle mayonnaise and halibut, and some crisp cabbage, are wrapped in hot corn tortillas for a delicious meal in your hands. Leftover cake is toasted and served with more fresh berries.

wednesday

CURRIED FISH SOUP WITH POTATOES, JALAPEÑOS, AND TOMATOES
Leftover halibut and potatoes are combined with clam juice, coconut milk, and Thai-inspired seasonings in an easy-to-assemble soup.

Fresh halibut is a lovely, mild, fairly soft-textured white fish. In this menu it is gently poached, then paired with a quick chipotle mayonnaise. Simple vegetables, steamed new potatoes, and braised baby bok choy are excellent accompaniments. Dinner is completed beautifully with a lemon–poppy seed cake accented with fresh berries.

The cake should be made the morning of serving to allow time for it to cool completely. The chipotle mayonnaise can be whipped together early as well. Final preparations are a snap. About thirty minutes before serving, steam the potatoes, then toss them with butter and herbs and keep warm. The halibut needs only ten to twelve minutes poaching time. While it is poaching, the bok choy braises.

The halibut is used twice during the ensuing week, once in some quick, everybody-put-their-own-together tacos, and in an Asian-inspired fish soup. The cake is lovely in any form again, but particularly nice toasted and topped with berries.

Poached Halibut with Chipotle Sauce

Serves 4, with half of the halibut and 1 cup sauce reserved for Halibut Tacos (page 150) and Curried Fish Soup with Potatoes, Jalapeños, and Tomatoes (page 151)

Halibut is a justifiably popular, mildly flavored fish that can be eaten unsauced, especially when grilled, but it also pairs well with sauces. Poaching, or cooking in simmering water, is the easiest method of cooking individually portioned pieces of fish. Since no added flavor results from this simple cooking technique, a rich and spicy sauce is perfect with the fish. Chipotle chilies (smoke-dried jalapeños) deliver the spiciness, while mayonnaise delivers the richness.

CHIPOTLE SAUCE:

2 cups mayonnaise

½ cup buttermilk

4 canned chipotle chilies in adobo sauce, minced

¼ cup minced fresh cilantro

½ teaspoon salt

2½ pounds halibut fillets, or 2¾ pounds halibut steaks

Fresh cilantro sprigs for garnish

TO MAKE THE SAUCE: Whisk all the ingredients together in a medium bowl.

Fill a large sauté pan or skillet with water to within 1 inch of the top. Bring the water to a simmer over medium-high heat. Measure the fish at its thickest part. Cook the fish in 2 or more batches. Slip the fish into the water, regulating the heat so that the water just bubbles slightly, and cook until just barely translucent in the center; an instant-read thermometer inserted on an angle into the fish will register 120° to 130°F. Timing will vary according to how the fish is shaped. A wide piece about 1 inch thick will take about 10 minutes, while a thicker piece will take longer. Use a slotted metal spatula or soup skimmer to gently lift the fish from the water and onto a platter.

When the last of the fish has been poached, pat the fish dry with paper towels. Remove any skin. If you purchased halibut steaks, gently separate the fish from the bones. Cut the fish into serving portions.

Set half of the fish aside to cool and place the rest on warm dinner plates. Reserve 1 cup of the chipotle sauce. Top each serving with about 2 tablespoons of the remaining sauce, garnish with cilantro sprigs, and serve. Pass the rest of the remaining sauce at the table. Wrap and refrigerate the reserved halibut and sauce for up to 4 days.

Steamed New Potatoes

Serves 4 (4 potatoes per person), with the rest reserved for Halibut Tacos (page 150) and Curried Fish Soup with Potatoes, Jalapeños, and Tomatoes (page 151)

It's such a treat when something as simple as a perfectly steamed potato can be so delicious.

38 small new red-skinned potatoes (about 4 pounds), each about 1½ inches in diameter, scrubbed

2 tablespoons unsalted butter, melted

⅓ cup minced fresh parsley

Salt and freshly ground pepper to taste

Fill the bottom pan of a 3-piece steamer pot (see Cook's Note) with 2 inches of water, cover with a tight-fitting lid, and bring to a boil. Put the potatoes in the steamer rack, set over the boiling water, cover, and adjust heat to maintain a slow boil. Steam the potatoes for 25 minutes, or until tender when pierced with a fork. In a large bowl, combine the hot potatoes, butter, and parsley. Add salt and pepper. Toss gently to mix.

Serve 4 potatoes per person and set aside the remaining potatoes to cool. Wrap the reserved potatoes well and store in the refrigerator for up to 4 days.

COOK'S NOTE   *If you don't own a 3-piece steamer pot, use an inexpensive, collapsible steamer rack. Add 2 inches of water to a large saucepan with a tight-fitting lid and steam as in the recipe.*

Stir-Fried Baby Bok Choy

Serves 4

Baby bok choy is often available in supermarkets these days. Large-stalked bok choy may be used for this recipe, but try the baby ones and taste how sweet and tender they are.

---

2 pounds baby bok choy, trimmed and
   halved lengthwise
2 tablespoons vegetable oil
2 tablespoons oyster sauce mixed with 3
   tablespoons water
1 tablespoon Asian sesame oil

Heat a wok or large skillet over high heat. Add the vegetable oil and swirl to coat the pan. Stir-fry the bok choy for 2 minutes. Add the oyster sauce mixture and stir-fry until the bok choy is crisp-tender, about 2 minutes. Add the sesame oil, stir to combine, then serve immediately.

Lemon–Poppy Seed Cake

Makes 12 servings

This cake, baked in a tube or Bundt pan, is at once tender and crunchy, thanks to the poppy seeds. After baking, a lemon sugar syrup is poured over the cake, further brightening its flavor. Easy to make, this cake freezes beautifully, and is a last-minute savior when you need a dessert on short notice.

CAKE:

- 1 cup (2 sticks) unsalted butter at room temperature
- 2 cups granulated sugar
- Minced zest of 3 large lemons (see Cook's Note)
- 3 large eggs at room temperature
- 1 cup buttermilk
- 3 cups all-purpose flour
- ½ teaspoon baking soda
- ½ teaspoon salt
- ¼ cup poppy seeds

TO MAKE THE CAKE: Preheat the oven to 350°F. Select a 10- or 11-inch tube or Bundt pan, preferably nonstick, and spray it with vegetable-oil cooking spray. In a large bowl, cream the butter, sugar, and lemon zest together until light and fluffy, using a wooden spoon or an electric mixer. Beat in 1 egg and one third of the buttermilk. Repeat twice to add the remaining eggs and buttermilk. In a medium bowl, whisk the flour, baking soda, salt, and poppy seeds together. Add to the wet ingredients and beat just until blended.

Use a rubber spatula to scrape the batter into the prepared pan. Smooth the top uniformly. Bake until a wire cake tester or toothpick inserted in the center comes out clean, about 50 minutes. Let cool in the pan for 30 minutes, then run a thin-bladed nylon spatula or dull knife around the edges of the cake to loosen it from the pan. Place a wire rack over the pan and hold it in place while turning the pan upside down and shaking it gently to unmold the cake. Let cool for 2 hours.

SYRUP:

- ⅔ cup fresh lemon juice (from 2 to 5 lemons, depending on their juiciness)
- ⅓ cup granulated sugar

TO MAKE THE SYRUP: In a 1-quart nonreactive saucepan, bring the lemon juice and sugar to a simmer over medium heat, stirring until the sugar dissolves. Continue simmering for 5 more minutes. Using a toothpick, poke holes in the cake in a random pattern about 1 inch apart. Using a pastry brush, brush the lemon syrup all over the cake until all the glaze is used.

COOK'S NOTE *Remove the zest from any citrus fruit by carefully peeling it off with a vegetable peeler or a sharp knife, leaving the bitter white pith underneath. Or, even easier, buy a citrus zester (it has a flat blade made up of 4 or 5 tiny round holes that strip off the zest) at a kitchenware shop; it makes the job a snap.*

Halibut Tacos

Serves 4

Flat breads, such as tortillas, make instant sandwich wraps for a wide variety of foods. If you have a few tasty leftovers in the refrigerator, and can figure how to combine them, a good dinner is at hand. In this recipe, leftover halibut, cut-up potatoes, and soft corn tortillas provide the basis for the meal. Thinly shredded cabbage lends its crunch, and a smoky, spicy chipotle sauce ties everything together. Serve all the components in bowls and let everyone make their own tacos.

10 Steamed New Potatoes (page 146), cut
    into ½-inch pieces
16 corn tortillas
8 ounces cabbage, thinly shredded
    (about 6 cups)
3 green onions, including green tops,
    thinly sliced
2 teaspoons fresh lemon juice
1 cup Chipotle Sauce (page 145)
2 cups ½-inch dice Poached Halibut
    (page 145) at room temperature

Preheat the oven to 200°F. Place the tortillas in a covered heatproof container such as a tortilla warmer or a shallow casserole with lid; put the potatoes in a similar container. Warm the tortillas and the potatoes in the oven for 15 minutes before serving.

In a medium bowl, toss the cabbage, green onions, and lemon juice together, then put in a serving bowl. Put the Chipotle Sauce in a serving bowl. Place the fish in a serving bowl.

Place the tortilla and potato serving containers on the table, along with the halibut, sauce, and cabbage mixture. Each diner takes a tortilla, spreads it with a little sauce down the middle, adds a little potato and a little fish, and garnishes the taco with some cabbage mixture.

Curried Fish Soup with Potatoes, Jalapeños, and Tomatoes

Serves 4

You won't believe how quickly this delectable soup goes together when you have leftover cooked fish and potatoes.

2 tablespoons vegetable oil

1 small yellow onion (about 3 ounces), cut into thin wedges

2 teaspoons curry powder

1½ cups water

1 bottle (8 ounces) clam juice

1 can (13½ ounces) unsweetened coconut milk

12 Steamed New Potatoes (page 146), quartered

2 jalapeño chilies, seeded and finely sliced (see Cook's Note, page 126)

1 tomato, cut in half vertically, cored, seeded, and cut into thin wedges

2 tablespoons fresh lime juice

1¼ cups flaked Poached Halibut (page 145)

Salt to taste

In a 3½- to 4-quart saucepan or Dutch oven over medium-high heat, heat the oil. Swirl to coat the pan, add the onion, and sauté until soft and lightly browned, 2 to 3 minutes. Add the curry powder and sauté until fragrant, about 30 seconds. Add the water, clam juice, and coconut milk. Stir to blend. Bring to a simmer, reduce heat to maintain a low simmer, and cook for 5 minutes.

Add the potatoes, jalapeños, tomato, and lime juice. Simmer for 5 minutes. Add the fish and heat through. Taste, add salt, and serve.

weekend

ROAST BREAST OF TURKEY
SPICY WHITE BEAN STEW WITH ROASTED RED PEPPERS
WALNUT BREAD
PEARS BAKED IN RED WINE

monday

BEAN SOUP WITH BACON AND OREGANO
The white bean stew becomes an appealing soup with the addition of some milk, bacon, and seasonings. Leftover walnut bread accompanies the soup.

wednesday

TURKEY CAESAR SALAD WITH WALNUT BREAD CROUTONS
Toasted walnut bread cubes and sliced roast turkey make a savory main-dish Caesar salad.

thursday

TURKEY TETRAZZINI
An American classic provides two nights of great spaghetti casserole dinners. This also freezes well.

Turkey is often relegated to Thanksgiving, but it offers such pleasing flavors that it should be utilized more often. A roasted turkey breast yields a manageable amount of leftovers. The sliced roast turkey is served on a spicy white bean stew. A savory and slightly rich walnut bread accompanies the meal, and elegant pears baked in red wine complete it.

Start the walnut bread early in the day of serving, since it needs to rise twice. Bake the pears while the bread is rising. About two hours before serving, start the white bean stew, then roast the turkey breast.

Three great meals come from this one. The turkey, walnut bread, and bean stew are all used again.

Roast Breast of Turkey

Serves 4 (1 to 2 generous slices each), with the rest reserved for Turkey Caesar Salad with Walnut Bread Croutons (page 160) and Turkey Tetrazzini (page 162)

Roasting a turkey breast is even easier than roasting a chicken, and the leftovers make terrific weeknight meals.

1 whole (double) turkey breast (4½ to 5 pounds)

¼ cup fresh lemon juice

½ cup olive oil

Salt and freshly ground pepper to taste

Leaves from 3 sprigs fresh rosemary (each about 3 inches long), minced

Leaves from 3 sprigs fresh thyme, minced

Preheat the oven to 375°F. Trim any visible fat from the turkey breast and discard the neck if included. Pat the turkey breast dry with paper towels. Line a roasting pan with aluminum foil for easy cleanup, or use a nonstick pan. Place a roasting rack in the pan and set the turkey breast on the rack.

In a 2-cup glass measure, thoroughly combine all the remaining ingredients. Pour the mixture inside and over the turkey breast, coating it well. Set the turkey breast skin-side up. Place the roasting pan in the lower third of the oven. Roast the turkey breast, basting every 20 minutes, until the juices run clear when a sharp knife is inserted into the thickest part of the breast, or when an instant-read thermometer, inserted in the same spot and not touching bone, registers 165°F, about 1¼ to 1½ hours. Remove the turkey breast from the oven, baste again, cover it loosely with aluminum foil, and let rest for 10 minutes before carving and serving.

Cut 1 to 2 generous slices per serving and set the remaining turkey breast aside to cool. Wrap the reserved turkey breast well and store in the refrigerator for up to 3 days.

Spicy White Bean Stew with Roasted Red Peppers

Serves 4, with 5 or 6 cups reserved for Bean Soup with Bacon and Oregano (page 159)

Small white beans, such as Great Northern or navy, are cheap, filling, and possess a richness of flavor that only gets better when augmented with herbs, vegetables, or meats. This meatless version serves as the bed for the turkey breast in this menu. Notice that the beans are not soaked. We have become convinced that soaking shortens the cooking time only a little, but results in more split beans.

1 pound small dried white beans, such as
   Great Northern or navy
2 large onions (10 to 12 ounces each)
3 medium carrots (about 12 ounces total)
1 rib celery
¼ cup olive oil
6 garlic cloves
2 serrano chilies or 1 jalapeño chili,
   seeded and thinly sliced
3½ cups Chicken Stock (page 23), or 2
   cans (14½ or 16 ounces *each*) low-salt
   chicken broth
1 can (14½ ounces) crushed tomatoes in
   juice
2 tablespoons minced fresh rosemary
   leaves, or 2 teaspoons dried rosemary
1 red bell pepper (6 to 8 ounces), roasted,
   seeded, and cut into medium dice (see
   page 61)
   Salt and freshly ground pepper to taste
½ cup minced fresh parsley

Pick over the beans, discarding any rocks or shriveled beans, and rinse in a colander. Chop half of 1 onion, half of 1 carrot, and all the celery. In a 4-quart or larger saucepan over medium heat, heat the olive oil and sauté the chopped vegetables until soft but not browned, about 5 minutes. Add the beans, garlic, chilies, stock or broth, tomatoes and juice, and rosemary. Bring to a boil over medium-high heat, then reduce heat to a gentle simmer, and cover. Cook for 1 hour and 15 minutes.

Cut the remaining onions into 1-inch wedges. Cut the remaining carrots into ½-inch rounds. Add the onions and carrots to the pot. Cook until the beans are tender but not mushy, about 30 minutes.

Add the bell pepper to the beans. Add salt and pepper. Ladle 1 to 1½ cups stew into each of 4 wide soup plates or bowls and top each portion with a little parsley. Cover and refrigerate the remaining stew for up to 7 days.

Walnut Bread

Makes 1 round loaf to serve and 1 to freeze for Turkey Caesar Salad (page 160) and Bean Soup with Bacon and Oregano (page 159)

This uncomplicated loaf has an affinity for bean soup, and makes nice croutons for the turkey Caesar salad. The walnut oil is available in most supermarkets or at specialty foods shops. Refrigerate the oil after opening it.

¾ cup lukewarm water (80°F)

1 teaspoon active dry yeast

1 cup all-purpose flour

3 cups (12 ounces) walnut pieces, toasted for 10 minutes in a preheated 350°F oven

1 cup lukewarm water (80°F)

1½ teaspoons active dry yeast

1 tablespoon salt

½ cup walnut oil

2 teaspoons ground pepper

4½–5½ cups all-purpose flour

In a large bowl, stir the water and yeast together. Let stand for 1 minute, then stir in the flour. Cover loosely with plastic wrap and let stand in a warm place until bubbly, about 1 hour.

Stir the walnuts, water, yeast, salt, walnut oil, and black pepper into the yeast mixture. Add 4 cups of the flour and stir well with a wooden spoon or mix with an electric mixer. Stir in enough of the remaining flour to make a slightly sticky dough, and turn the dough out on a floured work surface. Knead the dough, adding sprinkles of flour as needed to prevent sticking, until smooth and elastic, about 5 minutes. Put the dough back in the bowl, cover, and let rise in a warm place until doubled in volume, 1 to 2 hours.

On a floured work surface, divide the dough in half. Deflate each piece and pull the edges into the center to create a round loaf, crimping the seam firmly. Place the loaves, seam-side down, on nonstick or parchment-lined baking sheets. Cover with a clean non-terry towel or oiled plastic wrap and let rise until doubled in volume, about 45 minutes.

Fifteen minutes before baking the bread, preheat the oven to 450°F. Just before baking, use a very sharp serrated knife or a razor blade to cut 2 or 3 slashes in the top of each loaf, about ½ inch deep. Put the bread in the oven, spray the oven walls with water about 6 times, and quickly close the door. Spray again after 5 minutes and again after 10 minutes. After 20 minutes, reduce the oven temperature to 400°F and bake until the breads are nicely browned. An instant-read thermometer inserted into the center of a loaf should read 200°F or higher. Let cool completely on a rack. Slice part of 1 loaf and serve. Place the second loaf in a large freezer bag and freeze for up to 3 months.

Pears Baked in Red Wine

Serves 4

This is simplicity itself. The pears bake in a special mixture of wine and maple syrup for two hours with only a few bastings. A bulb baster is a handy tool to have, but you can just use a spoon if you don't have one.

4 firm unpeeled Bosc or Anjou pears
1 cup red Zinfandel wine
½ cup maple syrup
1 teaspoon pure vanilla extract
½ teaspoon ground nutmeg
1 strip lemon zest, about ¼ inch wide and 1½ inches long
Pinch of salt

Preheat the oven to 300°F. Trim the base of each pear to allow it to stand upright. Combine all the remaining ingredients in a 9- or 10-inch glass pie plate. Stand the pears in the wine mixture.

Bake for 2 hours, basting the pears with the pan juices every 30 minutes or so. Transfer the plate to a rack to cool. Serve warm or chilled, with the pan juices.

Bean Soup with Bacon and Oregano

Serves 4

Since you've already made the bean stew, most of your work is already done. If you want a vegetarian soup, skip the bacon and use 1 tablespoon olive oil to sauté the garlic. Serve this with some of the leftover walnut bread or another crusty loaf.

5–6 cups Spicy White Bean Stew with
    Roasted Red Peppers (page 156)
2 cups milk
4 slices bacon, cut crosswise in ¼-inch-
    wide pieces
2 large garlic cloves, minced
2 teaspoons dried oregano
½ cup lightly packed fresh parsley leaves,
    coarsely chopped
½ teaspoon salt
    Freshly ground pepper to taste

In a blender or food processor, purée the bean stew and milk, in batches if necessary.

In a 4-quart saucepan over medium heat, sauté the bacon until almost crisp. Add the garlic and sauté until the bacon is crisp, 2 to 3 minutes. Using a slotted spoon, remove the bacon and garlic to a plate. Pour off all but 1 tablespoon of the bacon fat. Pour the bean purée into the pan and add the bacon mixture and oregano. Bring the soup to a boil over medium-high heat, stirring to prevent the soup from sticking and burning. Reduce heat so that the soup just simmers, cover, and cook for 5 minutes. Add the parsley, salt, and pepper. Serve.

Turkey Caesar Salad with Walnut Bread Croutons

Serves 4

One of the great things about having leftover bread is that you can turn it into croutons. Caesar salad is popular because of its rich flavors set against the crispness of romaine lettuce. Walnut bread croutons and roast turkey make this a salad worthy of starring as an entrée.

½ loaf Walnut Bread (page 157), cut into
   ¾-inch cubes
2 large garlic cloves, minced
1 cup mayonnaise
1 tablespoon fresh lemon juice
3 tablespoons buttermilk or nonfat milk
1 tablespoon anchovy paste
   Leaves from 2 heads romaine lettuce,
   torn into bite-sized pieces (see Cook's
   Note)
½ cup (2 ounces) grated Parmesan cheese
4 slices Roast Breast of Turkey (page 155),
   cut into ¼-inch strips
   Freshly ground pepper to taste

Preheat the oven to 350°F. Spread the bread cubes on a baking sheet and toast in the oven until crunchy, about 20 minutes. In a small bowl, whisk the garlic, mayonnaise, lemon juice, buttermilk, and anchovy paste together. Put the croutons, romaine, Parmesan, and turkey in a large bowl. Add the pepper and dressing and toss thoroughly. Serve.

COOK'S NOTE   *Some romaine heads are simply huge, in which case 2 may be a little too much lettuce. Use your own judgment about whether to use all of both heads. Remember to use a salad spinner or paper towels to dry the lettuce after washing so water on the leaves doesn't dilute the dressing.*

Turkey Tetrazzini

Serves 4, with half reserved for another meal

Made correctly and with quality ingredients, this old-fashioned dish is classic comfort food. It takes a little longer to make than some of our other leftover recipes, but it makes enough for two meals.

2½ teaspoons salt
12 ounces spaghetti
6 tablespoons unsalted butter
6 tablespoons all-purpose flour
3 cups Chicken Stock (page 23) or
    canned low-salt chicken broth
¾ cup heavy (whipping) cream
    Freshly ground pepper to taste
2 teaspoons minced fresh rosemary
1 tablespoon minced fresh thyme
¼ teaspoon ground nutmeg
3½ cups ½-inch dice Roast Breast of Turkey
    (page 155)
10 ounces frozen green peas
½ cup dried bread crumbs
½ cup (2 ounces) grated Parmesan cheese

Fill an 8- to 10-quart stockpot three-fourths full with water, cover, and bring to a boil. Add 2 teaspoons of the salt to the stockpot. Add the spaghetti and cook until al dente (cooked through but still slightly chewy), 8 to 10 minutes. Drain, rinse under cold water, and set aside.

Preheat the oven to 375°F. Butter a 9-by-13-inch baking dish. In a 10-inch sauté pan or skillet, melt the butter over medium heat. Add the flour and stir until faintly colored, about 2 minutes. Gradually whisk in the stock or broth until the sauce is smooth and thickened, 3 to 5 minutes. Stir in the cream, then the remaining ½ teaspoon salt, the pepper, rosemary, thyme, and nutmeg. Taste and adjust the seasoning. Stir in the turkey and peas, heat through, and remove from heat.

Put the pasta in the prepared dish and spoon the turkey mixture over. In a small bowl, combine the bread crumbs and Parmesan. Sprinkle evenly over the sauce. Bake, uncovered, until heated through and bubbly, about 20 minutes. Preheat broiler and quickly brown the top of the casserole. Serve half of the casserole immediately and set the rest aside to cool. Cover the reserved casserole with plastic wrap and store in the refrigerator for up to 2 days.

The exact equivalents in the following tables have been rounded for convenience.

Liquid/Dry Measures

U.S.	METRIC
¼ teaspoon	1.25 milliliters
½ teaspoon	2.5 milliliters
1 teaspoon	5 milliliters
1 tablespoon (3 teaspoons)	15 milliliters
1 fluid ounce (2 tablespoons)	30 milliliters
¼ cup	60 milliliters
⅓ cup	80 milliliters
½ cup	120 milliliters
1 cup	240 milliliters
1 pint (2 cups)	480 milliliters
1 quart (4 cups, 32 ounces)	960 milliliters
1 gallon (4 quarts)	3.84 liters
1 ounce (by weight)	28 grams
1 pound	454 grams
2.2 pounds	1 kilogram

Length

U.S.	METRIC
⅛ inch	3 millimeters
¼ inch	6 millimeters
½ inch	12 millimeters
1 inch	2.5 centimeters

Oven Temperature

FAHRENHEIT	CELSIUS	GAS
250	120	1/2
275	140	1
300	150	2
325	160	3
350	180	4
375	190	5
400	200	6
425	220	7
450	230	8
475	240	9
500	260	10